TEACHING ENGLISH IN THE NATIONAL CURRICULUM

LEARNING THROUGH TALK AND EXPERIENCE:
THE ROLE OF DRAMA IN THE NATIONAL CURRICULUM

TEACHING ENGLISH IN THE NATIONAL CURRICULUM

LEARNING THROUGH IMAGINED EXPERIENCE:
THE ROLE OF DRAMA IN THE NATIONAL CURRICULUM

Jonothan Neelands

Series Editor: Patrick Scott

Hodder & Stoughton

LONDON SYDNEY AUCKLAND

ACKNOWLEDGMENTS

I am grateful to Nottinghamshire Dance and Drama Support Service and to all who sailed in and with her for providing the climate and enthusiasm which has nurtured this book.

British Library Cataloguing in Publication Data

Neelands, Jonothan
  Learning through imagined experience.
  – (Teaching English in the National Curriculum)
  I. Title   II. Series
  822.0071

  ISBN 0–340–54258–6

First published 1992

Produced by Serif Tree, Kidlington, Oxon
Printed in Great Britain for the educational publishing division of Hodder & Stoughton Ltd, Mill Road, Dunton Green, Sevenoaks, Kent by St Edmundsbury Press

CONTENTS

Introduction

Drama is not simply a subject, but also a method . . . a learning tool. Furthermore, it is one of the *key* ways in which children gain an understanding of themselves and of others.

Planning for drama in the classroom requires a clear understanding of its nature and the contribution it can make to children's learning. Drama is not simply confined to one strand in the statements of attainment which ceases after level six. *It is central in developing all major aspects of English. (English for ages 5–16)*

▰▰ Definitions and challenges ▰▰

This book aims to help teachers in Key Stages 2 and 3 to make the most of drama's potential to enhance a range of curriculum experiences, including language activities, for young people. The book is written partly as a practical response to the important and far ranging references to the need for drama in the National Curriculum documentation and partly in the knowledge that many teachers remain hesitant about initiating drama activities even though most would credit its value in learning. This paradox deepens when one considers that it is often the most valuable facets of drama which lead to the greatest hesitation on the teacher's part. The purpose of this introduction is, therefore, to clarify the value of drama, address the difficulties many teachers encounter in using drama and analyse what drama represents as a way of learning.

Many teachers remain confused about what actually 'counts' as drama, there is an apparently bewildering range of activities from staging plays, through games and improvisation to the kind of simulation or role-play encountered in INSET and training which also claim to be 'drama'. Some clarity of definition is to be found in the HMI document *Drama 5–16*:

Drama in schools is a practical artistic subject. It ranges from children's structured play, through classroom improvisations to performances of Shakespeare. It relies on the human ability to pretend to be someone or something else. Through this act of the imagination, pupils can explore how people in particular circumstances might behave now and at different times and in different societies. Though imaginary, the exploration can be experienced and shared as if it were real.

Through drama we recreate and examine people's actions, including our own, and see both how they might have come about and where they might lead. We test our individual viewpoints against those of others; this is what happens as soon as two people take on different roles in a drama. They are placed in opposition, or at the very least they represent different points of view. The conflicts at the heart of drama carry the process forward. By testing and, where possible, resolving human predicaments, drama helps pupils to face intellectual, physical, social and emotional challenges.

It follows from this definition that drama is a broad and encompassing term that associates a rich variety of ways of working which have as their common element the human ability to imagine and re-create other people's behaviour at other times and in other places. The definition itself prompts a list of the features of drama most frequently considered valuable by teachers and students alike.

Drama is a practical activity

It allows young people the opportunity to use space and movement, in addition to speech, in order to make meanings. It is not desk bound or dependent on the ability to write for its expression. It is an apparently loose and fluid form which in fact requires discipline and constraint for its execution.

But . . . because it is practical and tends to use large spaces the problems of management and control are more complex than in conventional 'desk-and-text-book' approaches to teaching.

Because drama uses words and human actions for its expression there tends to be no written record as evidence of 'work'. *Even though follow-up work in other curriculum areas may serve as evidence that the drama has enhanced young people's understanding,* many teachers are pressured to produce written outcomes or results for all classroom activity, or to look upon learning which is difficult to assess precisely as being of secondary importance.

Drama is a form of shared cultural activity

It is part of an unbroken cultural tradition which has been present in all civilisations throughout history. Sharing in cultural experiences is one way in which the young become initiated into the values, traditions and identity of their society. This has become an increasingly urgent argument for drama, and other arts, in schools given that technological progress has generally led to a decline in opportunities for shared cultural activity in society as a whole. The effects of TV, changes in food technology, the dangers of being on the streets, the prevalence of recorded music in public places and the automation of retailing and industry have all resulted in: less playing and singing and dancing and storytelling in the home and in public places; less live community culture; less human interaction in the home, streets and shops; less distinctive, cultural representation for minorities and local communities.

But . . . the notion that schooling provides young people with an induction into society through cultural involvement is not a priority for the present government and its educational legislation. It is therefore difficult for teachers to argue this cultural priority against the government's priority of basic and vocational training in preparation for fulfilling an economic role.

Drama provides a vehicle for exploring human nature and experience

It does this through accessible and concrete examples ('stories-in-action') which serve to provide young people with the means to express their own experience and to develop central societal concepts such as democracy, justice and freedom as well as personal concepts such as love, relationships, and family. Because the 'stories-in-action' which are the content of drama are composed out of the negotiations and understandings of those taking part, the teacher needs to develop the skills of a story teller who is able to select content, form, register and tone and develop a story from the responses of the group and her understanding of their potential for achievement.

But . . . language specialists, in particular, are often trained in and attracted to more private forms of fiction making, reading, writing etc. which do not involve the same level of social interaction and teacher responsiveness. Drama is a *social and collective art form* with very different demands for students and teachers alike.

Drama involves taking on roles and adopting different viewpoints in 'real' experiences

Encouraging students to work through dramatic situations, in fictitious roles, enables them to view their own behaviour, and other people's, from unfamiliar perspectives. The emotional experience is real for the students even though the activity is fictional (think, for example, of the real sadness that may move us when we read a story). As a consequence, the students can be helped to reflect on their behaviour in the drama from 'another' person's point of view. The right choice and management of situations, contexts and stories relating to the environment, for instance, can provide young people with authentic experiences of what it would be like to be in a threatened environment which may be far removed in time and place from their own immediate and protected environment (see p. 43). This is useful in overcoming the detached climate of the classroom by helping students: to see the underlying human significance and themes in their learning; to explore prejudices and stereotypes; to develop empathy and respect for others who are culturally, historically or socially different from themselves.

But . . . because drama often uses 'stories' in order to look at reality (history, social issues, relationships), there may be some concern about the legitimacy of what is learnt through drama, which may be more to do with subjective responses and 'feelings' rather than acquiring hard, objective facts. Some teachers are also concerned about the depth of feelings some young people may experience through drama which may touch upon realities in a young person's life that the teacher is not trained to support. As the definition from *Drama 5–16* suggests, drama inevitably pivots around conflicts of principle, values, attitudes. This means that, quite rightly, the stories in drama often provoke discussion about morality and reality. Often students will take a strong stand in relation to their feelings about justice and fairness in the 'stories' they engage with.

There is understandable concern about what might be the most supportive teaching strategy for dealing with the expression of a range of deeply felt values and convictions in the classroom. This is particularly important at a time when there are so many divisions in society, represented within our classrooms, which occur on the basis of gender, race, class, creed and belief. There is also constant concern about ideological bias, partisan imbalance and teacher accountability which are all associated with learning about reality through fiction.

Drama generates vocal and active responses to fictional situations
Learning in drama results from facing the challenge of behaving realistically in a fictional situation and then being pressed by the circumstances of the fiction, as it unfolds, into finding and using appropriate vocal and active responses. It is this 'realness' of drama, in which role-players give and receive (write and read) each other's messages simultaneously, which makes drama a unique form of literacy. In conventional reading and writing activity, fictional situations are unalterable, recorded and described; students are either fixed in the role of spectator, observer or reader, or in the role of writer. In drama the same fictions may be transformed by the students' responses, and the fictions are entered into and lived as a 'here and now' experience. This immediacy prompts new understandings and uses of language as a direct result of the active experiencing of the fiction.

But . . . the potential contribution of drama to literacy development has tended to be ignored beyond Key Stage 1. The Statutory Orders for English make only token reference to drama's usefulness in providing practice for oracy skills whilst legislating for a plethora of conventional approaches to language development which may break literacy into discrete areas such as spelling, reading etc.

Each of these areas has its packages of skills and Programmes of Study which do not sufficiently stress whole-language experience, or integrated approaches to literacy. Faced with the weight of detail in the Statutory Orders, and uncertain about drama's potential, many teachers are reluctant to take time from what they must teach, by law, in order to teach as they might want to, i.e. by using ways of working which are non-statutory.

Drama develops the imagination's ability to 'make believe'
Drama develops the imagination's ability to construct and 'make believe' unfamiliar contexts and situations; it demands that we respond to them as if they were actually occurring. In drama young people are able to take satisfaction in creating credible and coherent, alternative worlds and experiences through their own imaginative efforts. In so doing, young people are realising and extending their ability to imagine new futures and alternatives, new problems and solutions, a world beyond the street corner. Drama encourages creative ways of understanding and offers young people an opportunity to express their developing view of human experience.

But . . . again the present climate of legislation tends to ignore the importance of the imagination in young people's learning. In an effort to create a skills-centred approach that will prepare young people for their economic roles after schooling, the National Curriculum pays scant attention to the importance of providing for the imaginative needs of young people as they are developing through childhood into adolescence. In so doing, the curriculum is in danger of being presented to young learners as stale facts and skills to be drilled in. Without due attention to the imagination, young learners are denied the sense of conflict, excitement, anticipation and satisfaction which accompanies both the discovery of learning and the difficult psychological passage from Key Stage 2 to Key Stage 3.

▬ *A model for language learning* ▬ *through story and play*

Drama is essential to the development of speaking and listening skills as well as providing a bridge for other forms of learning in literacy, such as reading and writing in a wide range of registers for one's own purposes. The role of drama in relation to reading fiction is well put in the DES document, *Aspects of Primary Education: Language and Literature*:

> . . . effective work in drama often uses literature to enrich children's first hand experience in imaginary situations, the immediacy of which stimulates them to adapt their language to their roles. Through drama, the children's language repertoire and their understanding can be extended in a unique way.

There is growing evidence which testifies to this power of drama in offering young learners a unique relationship with literature and talk. Using drama, a child is able to enter into the world of a book or story and behave as one of its characters, free to ask other characters (taken on by the teacher and others in the group) the questions that they want to ask and free to attempt to negotiate alternative choices to those given in the original. The difference in comprehension is similar to the difference between hearing about an event and acutally being there at the time. Drama therefore complements and enhances other creative forms such as reading and writing, and by including drama with other creative forms a teacher is able to offer all young people a tool for expression. This enhancement means that a broader range of ability has access to an expressive form.

However, in terms of the whole curriculum – which includes language – this book claims that drama is an important way of *enhancing* classroom learning: it is not a substitute for analysis, objective learning and pastoral counselling; rather, it provides a bridge between the unfamiliar world of concepts and data and the recognisable world of human experiences and endeavours. The argument for *drama* in the classroom is like the argument for fiction, generally, which Harold Rosen expresses as:

> Narrative [*drama*] must become a more acceptable way of saying, writing, thinking and presenting. I am not proposing that anecdote [*drama*] should drive out analysis but that narrative [*drama*] should be allowed it's honourable place in the analysis of everything, that stories-in-the-head [*in-action*] should be given their chance to be heard. (*Stories and Meanings*)

Despite the strength of these arguments in favour of drama as an active learning tool with a broad range of applications within and beyond the language curriculum, there are apparent 'risks' involved in using drama. As teachers, we all face this dilemma of wanting to work in lively and inspiring ways with young people whilst also needing the professional security of remaining responsible and in control over classroom management. Many teachers feel unsupported by pre-service and in-service training in the non-specialist uses of drama.

Risk 1   Whether or not the cost in time and energy expended in developing drama will find a return in improved standards across a broad range of abilities.

Risk 2   Whether using drama might lead to a feeling of losing control and purpose.

Risk 3   Whether or not, as experience of using drama grows, the teacher and a group will become more effective at encountering the problems of planning and managing the drama together.

(Chapter 4 gives practical advice on how to reduce the risks and maximise the potential of managing and planning drama in Key Stages 2/3.)

Whilst suggestions can be made as to how the risks identified above can be reduced, and gaps left by inadequate training opportunities can be plugged, the problem of 'cost' – the time and energy expended in developing drama opportunities – remains. As with other forms of innovative and active learning, a teacher's decision to adopt drama into her repertoire of teaching styles will largely depend on the teacher's own value system. There are clear similarities between drama and the kinds of approaches associated with 'real' reading, developmental writing and the best practice in early-years education.

These approaches are characterised by a view of language learning which goes beyond the superficial acquisition of skills and linguistic conventions and terminology to consider the relationships between language and thought, language and social context and language and identity. In other words, they amount to a view of learning which recognises the centrality of language to all human activity and which seeks to develop a young person's language as a tool for socialising, thinking, communicating, expressing emotions, forming ideas and action etc.

Within this view, drama is an important means of constructing and experiencing the social contexts within which the different functions and uses of language can be identified and developed. The practical advice offered in this book is generally to do with building and working in dramatic 'social contexts' which offer the possibility for a richer variety of language and learning experiences than would be possible in a 'skills-and-drills' approach.

The view of language learning outlined in Figure 1 is considered, in this book, in relation to Key Stage 2 and Key Stage 3 but it is influenced by understandings about the nature of language acquisition which have their widest currency in approaches to Key Stage 1.

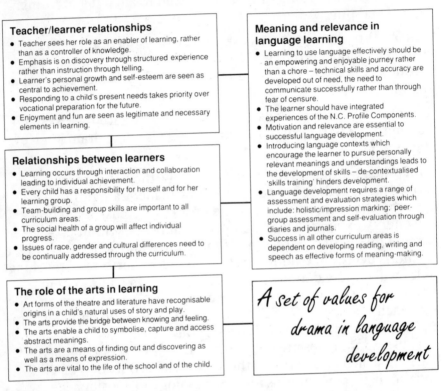

Teacher/learner relationships
- Teacher sees her role as an enabler of learning, rather than as a controller of knowledge.
- Emphasis is on discovery through structured experience rather than instruction through telling.
- Learner's personal growth and self-esteem are seen as central to achievement.
- Responding to a child's present needs takes priority over vocational preparation for the future.
- Enjoyment and fun are seen as legitimate and necessary elements in learning.

Relationships between learners
- Learning occurs through interaction and collaboration leading to individual achievement.
- Every child has a responsibility for herself and for her learning group.
- Team-building and group skills are important to all curriculum areas.
- The social health of a group will affect individual progress.
- Issues of race, gender and cultural differences need to be continually addressed through the curriculum.

The role of the arts in learning
- Art forms of the theatre and literature have recognisable origins in a child's natural uses of story and play.
- The arts provide the bridge between knowing and feeling.
- The arts enable a child to symbolise, capture and access abstract meanings.
- The arts are a means of finding out and discovering as well as a means of expression.
- The arts are vital to the life of the school and of the child.

Meaning and relevance in language learning
- Learning to use language effectively should be an empowering and enjoyable journey rather than a chore – technical skills and accuracy are developed out of need, the need to communicate successfully rather than through fear of censure.
- The learner should have integrated experiences of the N.C. Profile Components.
- Motivation and relevance are essential to successful language development.
- Introducing language contexts which encourage the learner to pursue personally relevant meanings and understandings leads to the development of skills – de-contextualised 'skills training' hinders development.
- Language development requires a range of assessment and evaluation strategies which include: holistic/impression marking; peer-group assessment and self-evaluation through diaries and journals.
- Success in all other curriculum areas is dependent on developing reading, writing and speech as effective forms of meaning-making.

A set of values for drama in language development

Figure 1 A set of values for Drama

In her influential research into the language development of preschool and infant children, the child psychologist Joan Tough identifies three *essential* conditions for successful learning:

- **Dialogue with an empathetic adult**
  Through drama the teacher is able to engage in dialogue with children in a variety of adult roles other than 'teacher': as someone who needs help; as someone who has had a special and exciting experience; as someone from a different culture or time; as someone who is struggling with a disability etc.

- **Opportunities for imaginative play**
  The spontaneous and unformed play of Key Stage 1 becomes more conscious and crafted through Key Stage 2 – Key Stage 3 so that whilst retaining some of the spontaneity of infant play there is a growing awareness of the art form and its possibilities.
- **An enabling environment that provides a variety of language experiences**
  Drama offers the possibility of building and working in a variety of different roles, situations, places, each of which provides new and authentic language demands within a secure environment.

Together these three conditions for learning seek to re-create in the classroom a model of learning which has been successfully operated by most pre-school children in acquiring the basics of a 'mother-tongue' (here used as a nurturing term, quite literally learning to use mother's tongue!). Researchers like Joan Tough have sought to understand the means by which young people undertake the most sophisticated and complex of all human learning achievements. In doing so, they have discovered that pre-school children use a range of behaviour and processes in order to satisfy their basic need to communicate with others and understand the world around them. The apparent success with which most of us manage this early learning has prompted attempts to preserve and develop the mother-tongue learning model into formal schooling. Here, for instance, is an extract from a document on assessment issued to schools by the Ministry of Education in Ontario, Canada:

> Today there is a growing conviction that 'most learning occurs not as a private, interior experience, but as an interactive one, socially shaped. Knowledge is less a personal acquisition than an inter-personal production: relational, collaborative and more specifically a matter of exchange. In fact the way children learn their mother tongue is seen as a potential model for all learning, and schools in many countries are now beginning to institutionalise this model. It places students at the centre of activity in the curriculum, and it emphasises learning not teaching. (*Does This Count?*)

In the present educational climate in this country, it is hard to imagine that governments in North America are beginning to put forward the view expressed above as a rationale for re-organising schooling. The example given above arrived in schools after seven years of working with a Provincial curriculum and testing system much like our own National Curriculum.

In these countries and others, there is a growing belief that too much emphasis has been given to what must be taught in schools and too little to understanding the processes which separate successful learners from less successful, and, in turn, to what are then the most effective processes for learners to use. This commitment to change the emphasis of government thinking results from a growing awareness that education cannot have the single aim of preparing young people for an economic role. For children's and society's sake, it must also prepare them for a broader social role; education must have an instrumental value, but not at the expense of its intrinsic value.

The model of mother-tongue learning is often echoed by language specialists writing about the organisation of language learning in later stages of education. Here is Nancy Martin talking about learning in Key Stages 2/3:

> In coming to understand how children learn language, we have come to understand that this is also the way of much other learning. In taking part in rule-governed behaviour – a meeting, a party, group discussion, dramatic improvisation and so on – a newcomer picks up the implied rules by responding to the behaviour of others and quickly internalises them. Becoming literate operates in a similar way. We learn what stories are by reading and telling and writing them; similarly with other genres. There is, of course the alternative, traditional mode by which teachers analyse the rules and teach them as procedures or models. (*The Word for Teaching is Learning*)

In her analysis, Nancy Martin is arguing for an interactive, contextual and social mode of language learning which seeks to develop the mother-tongue model. Figure 2 attempts to represent this model graphically so as to remind us of the key features of learning:

- The child is at the centre of her learning; there is no formal external curriculum for her to comply with. The motivation and purpose for learning is borne out of her *need* to communicate not just her immediate physical needs, but her thoughts, dreams, fears and hopes.
- The child learns through interaction with those around her – parents, siblings, peers, the wider community etc. She also learns through interaction with TV, books, pictures, songs and rhymes, pets etc.

- The child uses a range of real behaviours in her learning, named in the upper semi-circle of the diagram. *But* she also uses a range of symbolic or representative forms in her learning which are named in the bottom semi-circle. It is this use of story, imaginative play, rhythm and other cultural activity in making sense of and explaining the world around her which is of particular significance in relation to drama and language development.
- Alongside the skills acquired in mother-tongue learning, children also develop knowledge about human nature. They are skilled observers whose principle concern is to understand how people behave, how to gain reward, how to get what they need and what happens when they or others behave in certain ways. *They are used to learning about the world from within the context of human behaviour.* They may also develop a strong affinity with the animal world through observing that animals too are in the power of adults, and not always successful in communicating their needs!

Figure 2 Mother-tongue learning

Readers of this book will undoubtedly be familiar with the importance of story and play in early-years learning but may be quizzical about the continuing significance of these forms in Key Stages 2/3.

Pre-school learning despite its complexity, is very concrete, actual and context bound. The types of real behaviour identified in the diagram are used to deal with what is actually present within the child's immediate horizons. The symbolic forms identified are used to help the child to begin to use language and behaviour to represent concepts, attitudes, behaviour, moods and feelings which are not concrete or present – in other words, to deal with the abstract world.

Through story and play, children can begin to make sense of a world which is invisible and distant until it is brought into the child's experience through symbolic language and action. Stories and play offer the child concrete examples of ideas and experiences, embedded in recognisable human situations, which they are too young to deal with through conceptual language and discourse.

In a conventional, transmission model of education, story and play are relegated to the sidelines when the curriculum begins to deal with increasingly abstract concepts and skills. Yet, story and play are the natural means by which young people process abstract thought. An alternative argument, based on common sense, would be to preserve the importance of story and play precisely because the curriculum becomes increasingly remote from real actions and concrete situations.

The more the curriculum requires children to operate at a symbolic level of concepts and generalisations which are divorced from particular situations, or from human experience, the more need they have for the support of story and play to help them understand and see the significance of their learning in recognisable contexts. In adult life we still have this same need for concreteness – think how much we communicate through story; how we prepare for difficult events by 'role-playing' the event in advance in our heads; how we would rather be shown how to fix our car than be told the theory of internal combustion!

The view of drama in this book is therefore rooted in a mother-tongue approach to learning in Key Stages 2/3. The content of the drama may be the key concepts, principles and generalisations which form the language curriculum and much more. The mode of learning attempts to re-create the *need* to learn through providing concrete examples of situations in which people find themselves actively using or discovering the importance of the content so that:

- content relating to the theme of buildings is taught through the situation of being builders needing to finish a construction (see p. 40).
- content relating to the theme of democracy and the difference between cultures is taught through the situation of the crowds standing for freedom in Tianamen Square (see p. 24).
- content relating to the environment is taught through the situation of scientists travelling to the North Pole to conduct experiments (see p. 43).

This mode of learning works successfully when the class and teacher are able to fuse:

STORY • PLAY • NATURE

drama

CHAPTER I

Drama as a Medium for Learning Talk

The National Curriculum stresses the importance of speaking
and listening skills both as important areas of development in
their own right and as essential components in the development
of reading and writing skills. Many language teachers have taken
this to be an affirmation of a long struggle over the last decade to
establish the centrality of oracy skills in the development of
literacy. Attainment Target 1 and the related Programmes of
Study firmly stress the need for young people to be given *practice*
in a wide range of talk contexts with particular reference to
audience and purpose. In so doing, constant reference is made to
the importance of drama in providing a concrete sense of *context
and purpose*.

> The statutory order for the teaching of English . . . reflects the
> view that drama should be used to provide opportunities for
> practising varieties of language in different situations. (*Drama
> 5–16*)

Other researchers, who like Joan Tough (see p. 10) have been
associated with mother-tongue learning in the early years, have
reminded us of the natural advantage we provide the learner
with when we create learning experiences in which the skills,
concepts and understandings are embedded in 'real life' contexts
– when we seek to show in context rather than tell out of context.
As Margaret Donaldson explains:

> It is when we are dealing with people and things in the context of
> fairly immediate goals and intentions and familiar patterns of
> events that we feel most at home. And when we are asked to
> reason about these things, even verbally and at some remove
> from them, we can often do it well. (*Children's Minds*)

The importance of embedding young people's learning in 'real
life' and meaningful contexts has been widely acknowledged in
other areas of literacy development. The past decade has seen
the emergence of the 'Real reading' approach which has asserted
that the development of reading skills is best accomplished
through student contact and engagement with real and entire

texts. A parallel development has occurred in the teaching of writing in which young people are encouraged to write for their own purposes for real audiences such as family, organisations, newspapers, and the wider community. But it has taken the National Curriculum to place the idea of 'Real talk' firmly on the agenda for language teachers, even though language specialists like Harold Rosen have reminded us that talk is embedded in social context in such a way that the act of talking becomes inseparable from the context in which it is occurring:

> The social context, as we call it, is not an arena in which we perform our dramas. It is the dramas themselves; people in action with each other and against each other, improvising the text as they proceed. (*Out There, or Where The Masons Went*)

Of course, much valuable classroom work in the area of oracy has gone on, but in most cases the focus for the development of talk has either been through small-group exploratory and problem-solving talk, or talk in the presentation mode, or spectator/observer talk, recalling and recording experiences through anecdotes. There has not often been an explicit attempt to develop a greater variety of talk experiences through *the creation of 'real life' talk contexts in which the student operates in action as a 'live' participant.*

Through emphasising the need for experiential approaches to the development of language, the National Curriculum begins to acknowledge the importance of preparing students for the demands of increasingly complex talk contexts in society (dealing with racial abuse, for instance, or negotiating through talk rather than through physical conflict). The rationale for this emphasis on practical and contextual approaches to oracy is simple to grasp. Figure 3 attempts to map out *some* of the situations in which young people may find themselves later in life and in which, as teachers, we would surely want them to be effective and confident talkers. This list cannot begin to be an exhaustive inventory of 'real life' situations requiring sophisticated oracy skills, but it serves to remind us of the kinds of experiences which language users need to be practised in.

Conventionally, language teachers have tended to introduce children to the kind of situations illustrated in Figure 3 through the experience of fiction. In other words, young people only encounter 'other people' in these situations through stories, film etc., though they may also share their own similar experiences through anecdote. Whilst these activities are invaluable in giving

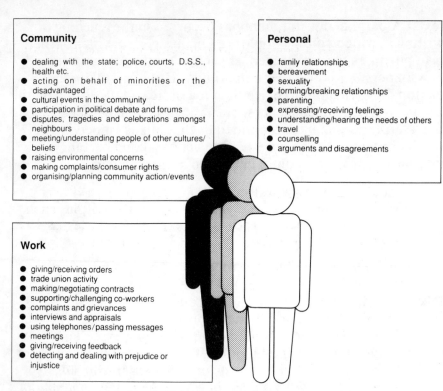

Community

- dealing with the state; police, courts, D.S.S., health etc.
- acting on behalf of minorities or the disadvantaged
- cultural events in the community
- participation in political debate and forums
- disputes, tragedies and celebrations amongst neighbours
- meeting/understanding people of other cultures/ beliefs
- raising environmental concerns
- making complaints/consumer rights
- organising/planning community action/events

Personal

- family relationships
- bereavement
- sexuality
- forming/breaking relationships
- parenting
- expressing/receiving feelings
- understanding/hearing the needs of others
- travel
- counselling
- arguments and disagreements

Work

- giving/receiving orders
- trade union activity
- making/negotiating contracts
- supporting/challenging co-workers
- complaints and grievances
- interviews and appraisals
- using telephones/passing messages
- meetings
- giving/receiving feedback
- detecting and dealing with prejudice or injustice

Figure 3 A sample of 'real life' talk demands

young people the chance to discuss and share – through anecdotes and stories – key, 'real life' experiences in the classroom, they do so at some distance from the real events and experiences they refer to. They do not give young people practical, concrete experience as *participants* who have to grapple with the emotions, tensions and nuances of behaviour which characterise 'real life' episodes; they restrict the learner to spectator/observer modes of language use, in other words, to recording, retelling, describing and witnessing.

Indeed, as long as young people and teachers restrict themselves and their talk to the real world of the classroom, the range of available contexts in which to explore the experience of 'real life' talk will remain narrow and confined to teacher–pupil, pupil–pupil talk within the context of school. If, on the other hand, teachers and young people are willing to use dramatic role-playing to help them imagine they are other than themselves, in another place and time, facing an imagined dilemma or experience as if it were actually occurring to them, then it becomes possible to re-create a potentially infinite variety of social contexts for talk. The involvement of the teacher in the drama adds the opportunity for the teacher to model register, vocabulary and tone as well as drawing out talk from the group (see Chapter 4).

Through working inside dramatic contexts as participants, young people can try out audiences, registers and respond to purposes which are clearly defined and bound to the context. They can respond to the context and test out a wide range of points of view in a real way, but, without having to suffer the consequences of their actions as they would do in life.

> In both improvised and text-bound drama, energy and conviction develop through the role or character adopted. This widens the emotional register and hence, the language required, whether it be the language of the courtroom, the interview, the quarrel, the conspiracy, the celebration, the farewell or any other dimension of the real or imagined world which children have constructed. (*Drama 5–16*)

In this sense, drama becomes essential to the development of oracy because it gives young people classroom experience of contexts which would otherwise remain inaccessible in the participant ('being there') mode of language use. James Britton, who has written extensively about the development of language in young learners, summarises the point:

> A dramatic situation that really takes hold in a group propels the members of it more forcibly out of their own skins into somebody else's than any other form of representation . . . drama is a special form of talking and doing . . . as a way of dealing with other times and places it is, as we have seen, more accessible than narration . . . in drama the situations and the actions within it are themselves represented, and the speech thus remains embedded, in contexts. (*Language and the Learner*)

To become powerful talkers, who are able to respond appropriately to audience and purpose, students need more than practice of talk in different contexts. They need also to be able to analyse contexts so that they are able to identify the key elements which will have a major bearing on what is said and how it will be heard. A difficulty is that any conceptual model of the relationship between utterance and context is going to be complex and difficult to communicate to students at an abstract, analytical level. This is particularly true for those young people who may have greatest difficulty in their own lives in successfully making sense of the requirements of social contexts. These students may also have difficulty in dealing with an abstract, conceptual and objectified approach to an area of experience which is already causing them anxiety.

Involving young people in negotiating, constructing and operating dramatic contexts is a particularly efficient means of giving them necessary and empowering insights into the relationship between context and language use and also an awareness of different registers and the development of a wide range of language skills.

Consider the difficulty of setting out to teach the model of the effect of social context on utterance in Figure 4 through traditional transmission modes of learning.

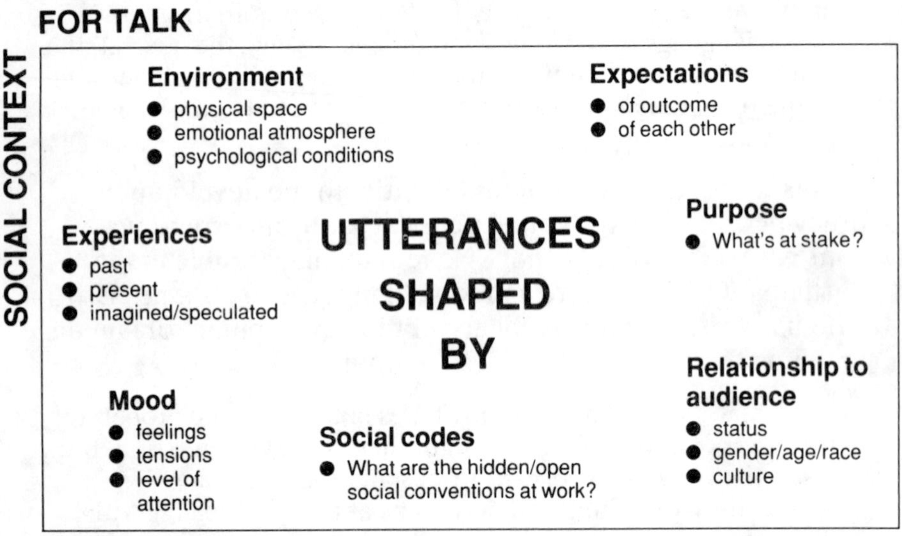

FOR TALK

SOCIAL CONTEXT

Environment
- physical space
- emotional atmosphere
- psychological conditions

Expectations
- of outcome
- of each other

Experiences
- past
- present
- imagined/speculated

UTTERANCES SHAPED BY

Purpose
- What's at stake?

Mood
- feelings
- tensions
- level of attention

Social codes
- What are the hidden/open social conventions at work?

Relationship to audience
- status
- gender/age/race
- culture

Figure 4 The effect of social context on utterance

Consider, also, how many young people have difficulty in detecting and understanding the range of social codes which govern the conventions of behaviour in certain contexts. Many young people encounter difficulties in their social lives precisely because they haven't accessed or recognised the need to respond to and manage the prevailing codes and conventions, even after a lifetime of parents and teachers *telling* them their behaviour/ manner is inappropriate for school, home, talking to parents, authority etc.

Even if a program were developed to teach knowledge of context at a conceptual level, students would not be given the *active experience* of the relationship between utterance and context. They would not be able to see, in concrete terms, how they, themselves, can effect and respond to the interrelationship between utterance and context. A drama approach, which combines experience as a participant – improvising in dramatically constructed social contexts –with reflection on *how* the experience is formed by the context, will begin to provide young people with insights into vital areas of human relationships.

In drama approaches, the problem of working with a largely conceptual model of context (see Figure 4) is overcome through the process of negotiating and constructing the context for dramatic improvisation, since a shared understanding of the context is necessary before dramatic action can take place. In constructing the context, those involved are naturally going to address the features of context outlined in the conceptual model as part of their *doing*. At one level, this will occur through responding to context-related questions such as:

In the drama . . .

- Who are we?
- Where are we?
- What is happening to us/between us?
- What time/period is it?
- What are we here to do?
- Has anything significant happened which has led us to this point?
- Where are we trying to get to?

It is natural in improvisation for those taking part to see the responses to these questions as forming the reason and the limits for the improvising that follows. In other words, the construction of context defines a specific social encounter and the improvisation itself will need to be authentic to the context – some reflective discussion will be to do with 'Would people really do/say that in this situation?'.

At another level, the process of dramatic improvisation itself will release deeper meanings and understandings of the context – utterance relationship. Young people will carry their own expectations of what will happen and what to say into an improvisation, but they will soon find themselves interacting with others whose expectation might be different. The need to respond to each other 'live' may help them to begin to realise the fuller implications of the situation, or they may be surprised, or pressed, into considering alternative views of the context and its embedded codes by the way others respond to their own communications. As David Booth puts it:

> In drama the students are allowed to talk themselves into believing in the fiction, to hear their ideas bounced back, to reframe and refocus their own information and attitudes, to recognise the need for communicating what they believe to those who believe differently, to actually hear language at work – changing themselves. Their words sweep them into thought, and as they recognise the truth of what they are saying, that very language is transformed into new patterns, it determines the action and lets them see the impact, all while they are in the midst of action, in the eye of the hurricane. (*Dramawords*)

Figure 5 represents a model of how language learning is processed in dramatic improvisation. (The model is adapted from *Some Use of Role Play as an Approach to the Study of Fiction, 8–14*, Bretton Language Development Unit.)

A MODEL OF LANGUAGE LEARNING THROUGH DRAMA

Figure 5

Planning for context-focussed drama

The theory of context and utterance emerging in this chapter may greatly assist teachers in the planning of drama work by providing a clear sense of purpose. The two examples of planning for context focussed drama that follow aim to demonstrate this. In each case, the teacher and class start with the idea of a key dramatic moment, or context (which may reflect the sorts of situations described in Figure 3, or might be 'borrowed' from a story), and then they build towards this moment through various imagined actions so that students are conscious of all the subtleties contained in the context and how their talk and experience in role will be shaped by the contextualising.

The development of the drama in each case will move through establishing a clear and accessible sense of the physical and temporal context which has been suggested towards an understanding of the social values and influences at work in the context. The dramas could have been even more closely focussed on experiencing the relationship between what is said and the particular contexts chosen if the groups had gone on to look at how even small changes in the context – a change of place, or emotional atmosphere, for instance – would have a corresponding change in effect on what was said. The acting out of the key moment is seen by the students as being the climax of their work so building towards that moment has particular interest and tension for them.

Example 1   After the Black Death (Key Stage 2)

- The class are working on the concept of feudalism and create a village community after the Black Death – some represent tenant farmers, others bondsmen. The different forms of taxation and tithing for both groups are demonstrated through the teacher's role of bailiff.
- Both groups prepare scenes to show the effect of taxation on their families, the hardship they suffer etc.
- The king announces, through the bailiff, a new tax on every head to raise much needed revenue to fight the French and to compensate for the loss of revenue caused by the decline in the population after the Black Death. The king declares that all must pay the same fixed amount.
- The families consider the fairness and effect of the new tax. As a whole group, they are invited to consider going directly to the king to put their case; they opt for this course of action.
- The key scene, therefore, is the meeting between the king and his people. This is built up slowly and carefully in order that the group is aware of the contextual elements identified in Figure 6. Once the group are aware – through questioning – of the situation, they improvise the talk of the common people confronting their ruler.

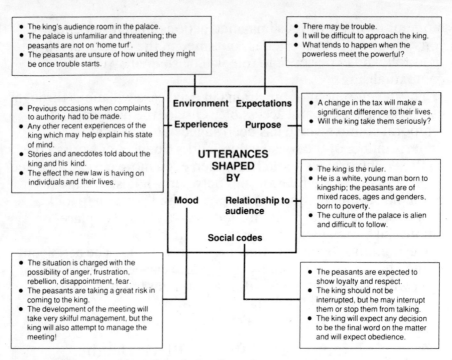

Figure 6 After the Black Death *Key Stage 2*

Example 2 Tianamen Square (Key Stage 3)

- Students work on their understanding of the events in Tianamen Square through looking at sets of colour photographs from Sunday Supplements. They are asked to select a key picture which best expresses the events for them and then to arrange the other photographs so as to build up to the key photograph.
- Students are introduced to a dilemma: the police have arrested a journalist for taking pictures of the army clearing the Square; the journalist is refusing to hand over the film and is being held in a police station close to the Square. A young consul is given responsibility for crossing the crowded Square to negotiate the journalist's release.
- A small group are given responsibility for creating the police station, complete with police, student prisoners and a detention room for the journalist. The remainder of the class work on the problem of simulating a 'crowd of a million' which the consul must pass through in order to get to the police station.

- The key moment is the consul's negotation with the police holding the journalist. The improvisation includes a volunteer in the role of the consul struggling through the crowds, entering the police station, and encountering an indifferent police officer who sends the consul back through the crowd to get some paperwork. The consul returns and meets the teacher in role as the journalist who has passed the film to a student hiding in the crowd. The journalist's top priority is to beat deadlines for publication of the photographs, which are seen by him as a route to international success. On leaving the station, the consul finds the teacher who has now taken on the role of the student with the film. The student tells the consul that the pictures must be used wisely as once they are published other students will be identified and arrested. The dilemma for the consul is what to do with the film when she returns to the police station, does she hand it over to the police, expose it, or substitute a fake and smuggle the 'real' film out of the country?

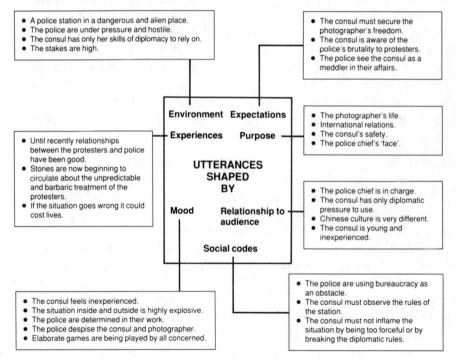

- A police station in a dangerous and alien place.
- The police are under pressure and hostile.
- The consul has only her skills of diplomacy to rely on.
- The stakes are high.

- The consul must secure the photographer's freedom.
- The consul is aware of the police's brutality to protesters.
- The police see the consul as a meddler in their affairs.

- Until recently relationships between the protesters and police have been good.
- Stories are now beginning to circulate about the unpredictable and barbaric treatment of the protesters.
- If the situation goes wrong it could cost lives.

Environment   Expectations

Experiences   Purpose

UTTERANCES SHAPED BY

Mood   Relationship to audience

Social codes

- The photographer's life.
- International relations.
- The consul's safety.
- The police chief's 'face'.

- The police chief is in charge.
- The consul has only diplomatic pressure to use.
- Chinese culture is very different.
- The consul is young and inexperienced.

- The consul feels inexperienced.
- The situation inside and outside is highly explosive.
- The police are determined in their work.
- The police despise the consul and photographer.
- Elaborate games are being played by all concerned.

- The police are using bureaucracy as an obstacle.
- The consul must observe the rules of the station.
- The consul must not inflame the situation by being too forceful or by breaking the diplomatic rules.

Figure 7 Tianamen Square *Key Stage 3*

CHAPTER 2

Exploiting the Symbolic Potential of Drama

> Literacy is . . . the ability to exploit the symbolic potential of language for one's own purposes (Gordon Wells, *Children as Meaning Makers*)

The depth of active inquiry into the key contexts described at the end of Chapter 1 suggests that there is something more for young people to gain from working in dramatic contexts beyond practising 'talk skills'. Dramatic contexts are not merely simulations of the real thing, they are formed and crafted representations of the real thing.

In simple terms, despite its immediacy and concreteness, drama sets out to make a thought-provoking *representation* of reality; it does not seek to duplicate or be a kind of 'virtual reality'. Dramatic contexts are in this sense no different from pictures, sculptures, films or poems. As with these other forms of art, we are drawn not just to the plot or content, but also to the form, to embedded meanings, to the metaphor. Drama is at its most powerful in developing talk when it sets out to reflect on the relationships between talk, thought and personal and social identity through using:

- **metaphor**   creating a representative example – dramatic context – in order to gain a broader understanding of a theme (e.g. *a particular trial scene may be used in order to broaden understanding of the theme of justice*).
- **symbols**   objects or icons which embody the meanings offered in the dramatic context (e.g. *a key which is a treasured possession because it unlocks a box of old letters; both objects come to represent a character's reluctance to face up to the past*).
- **role**   a range of invented viewpoints chosen to offer a particular frame on the scene so that young people experience the drama from an unfamiliar or fresh perspective which is either different from their own conventional view of a situation, or different from the view conventionally given in the media or elsewhere (e.g. *as judge, defense counsel, defendant, juror, victim, etc.*).

- **emotions**   Dramatic contexts tend to focus on and emphasise the emotions contained in a situation. As in other forms of fiction, the level of emotional entanglements, dilemmas and tensions may be in excess of what you could reasonably expect to have to suffer, simultaneously, in reality! But the pull of emotion leads to concern and thought as well as providing motivation – young people's obsession with the 'emotions' of soap-opera are testimony to the relationship between affective interest and student interest.

For example, the defendant's father may decide to give evidence for the prosecution whilst his mother offers to give evidence for the defence; the tension between them may be explored through the particular context of the mother and father sitting alone, in silence, outside the courtroom waiting to give evidence. What will they say, or not say, to each other? What goes through their minds (monologues)? What pictures do they have in their minds of the past (see **17 'Still images'**, p. 57)?

By being aware of the level of symbols, metaphor, role and emotions during drama, as they might be at a similar level when reading and writing stories, young people are able to gain a range of learning goals beyound developing talk skills. In particular: 'Drama . . . enables children to reconsider their feelings and attitudes in the light of shared experience' (*English Non-Statutory Guidance*). To see drama, therefore, merely as a method of simulating environments for talk, as the descriptions in the National Curriculum orders tend to, would be to ignore its power as an immediate and accessible symbolic form which young people can use together to represent, try out, interrogate and express key areas of human experience. The medium for doing so is *talk*.

▬ *Dramatic contexts for talk* ▬

In order to understand the importance of drama as a meaning-making process as well as being a vehicle for the development of oracy, there follow two short examples of drama which are designed to offer a variety of talk demands within a single thematic context: 'Jack and the Beanstalk' (Key Stage 2) and 'Disability' (Key Stage 3).

These examples serve to remind us that drama is not to do with naming a social context and then talking as if it were happening around us. The apparent paradox of drama is that it allows us on the one hand to get very close to the 'real thing' but on the other hand it is, as I have suggested, a symbolic representative form which allows us to *construct* and *depict* deliberately both the appearance of social situations and also the underlying themes and emotions.

In this way, drama is like poetry, prose and other language art forms in the sense that it mediates real experience through symbolic form and in so doing becomes both a representation and also a commentary, or vehicle for the group's and/or teacher's view of reality. The difference between drama and other language art forms is to do with the social and interactive nature of expression (it is created socially and publicly not individually and privately as is the case with poetry), and the immediacy and concreteness of its representations: it uses concrete actions and situations rather than symbolic language conventions.

The young people involved in the examples of dramatic contexts for talk are experiencing the talk as if it were a real occurrence, but at the same time they are conscious that their own behaviour and talk and that of the others involved is actually symbolic and only representative of the real thing: it's 'make believe'. Drama is a means of symbolically transforming an area of human experience into a construction which is concrete, accessible and familiar; it feels real but it's not! In this sense, drama is no different from any other representative, narrative art form – both the examples given are, in effect, fictional situations involving specific talk demands like the examples we might find and use in novels and stories – the difference is that young people engage with, and learn through, drama as *participants* in the imagined action not as spectators and observers of it as they would be in relation to examples drawn from story or film.

▬ Example 1   Jack and the Beanstalk ▬

A Year 6 class are involved in looking at folk tales from different cultures. During work on Jack and the Beanstalk the class are invited to consider three situations:

● What kind of market did Jack go to where he could exchange a cow for magic beans? What other goods were for sale? How would the traders have tried to persuade Jack to part with his cow?

In groups, the class erect stalls selling everything from seven league boots to magic carpets. They work at re-creating the atmosphere of the market – the cries of the traders etc. Then the teacher, in role as Jack, goes from stall to stall asking for explanations and demonstrations of the goods. When she comes to the trader of magic beans the whole class are invited to add to the trader's persuasion until finally Jack makes a trade.

● How will Jack tell his mother that all he has are the beans? The class represent the kitchen in Jack's house, a child takes the role of Jack's mother. The teacher is Jack and she asks the other children, who are watching, for advice on how best to approach mum, and how best to deal with her disappointment and anger. For many young people this is a familiar experience! They have little difficulty in advising Jack on how to read and respond to the situation and how best to use talk to escape a beating!

● Later in the drama, the class decide to go and 'kill' the giant. When they reach the top of the beanstalk they meet a kindly woman who turns out to be the giant's mum. She is very worried about her clumsy, giant son who doesn't know his own strength and keeps damaging things and hurting people because of his unusual size. Have the visitors seen him? Have they any advice? Isn't it terrible the way the world is going? The class quietly hide their weapons and sit with the giant's mum sharing advice on how to deal with difficult adolescents over a cup of tea!

▬ Example 2   Disability ▬

The teacher initiates a drama about images of teenage disability and relationships between people of different abilities in the following way:

● An empty chair is placed in a circle, the group are asked to imagine that the chair is a wheelchair seen by its owner, John, as a possible block to him being as free as others. The teacher enters the circle in the role of Julie, a friend of John. She reads an imaginary letter and asks the group to assess the relationship. The letter tells John that Julie is unhappy with the relationship and feels pressured, as a result she is telling John she won't go with him to a party on Saturday.

- The teacher has composed and read the letter so that it creates possible ambiguities about Julie's motives for deciding not to go to the party with John. Is it because she is embarrassed about their relationship when her friends are around? Is it because she is struggling to find the courage to deepen her relationship with John? Is it because John has spoilt a friendship by expecting more emotional commitment from Julie than she is prepared to give?

- The group enact a variety of scenes through spontaneous improvisation to select and explore key moments which might reveal these ambiguities. Spectators have the opportunity to stop the action and comment on what is being revealed in the improvisations; role-players are encouraged to reflect on their feelings as they respond in role to each other. Situations that might be improvised include:

  - Julie and John meeting Julie's friends whilst out shopping
    This might be used to explore Julie and her friends' attitudes to John.
  - Julie and John alone in John's house
    This might be used to explore what Julie means by 'being pressured'.

- The teacher maintains the role of Julie in order to sustain the ambiguities and develop them in response to the students' handling of the situations. Various members of the group take the roles of John and others in each scene and are challenged/supported by the teacher, both in role as Julie and out of role as facilitator, as to the image of John they project and what kind of talk and action is appropriate to the inquiry and dilemma.

- The drama culminates in the party. The group decide on where John and Julie are placed. The party is improvised. The teacher uses her role of Julie as a way of encouraging the group to reconcile their understanding of the relationship. The class assume their roles as guests at the party, interacting with each other and with John and Julie.

Figure 8 sets out to explain the differences between the modes of talk in conventional discussion, or a sharing of stories, about the talk contexts given in the examples above – buying and selling, facing an angry parent, breaking a relationship, facing up to a difficult meeting – as opposed to talking within a symbolic representation of the context (dramatic context).

Discussion mode
● talking about situations

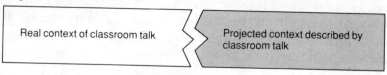

Drama mode
● talking within a representation of the situation

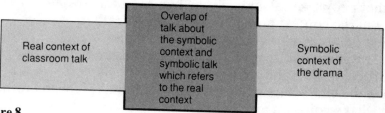

Figure 8

In discussion mode, some talk would be related to the real dimension of the classroom – giving instructions, explaining and negotiating – and some talk would be *about* the chosen topic for discussion, talking about unwanted relationships, for example. In discussion, the talk about the context will always be projected and based on prior observations and experiences. There will always be a difference, for both speakers and listeners, between the real context for talk which belongs to the classroom (participant language) and the reported and projected talk relating to an external context (spectator/observer language). In order to engage with the discussion, young people must either have had real experiences in similar contexts or be able to project into a context without the support and enhancement of accompanying action or representation, which the symbolic potential of drama provides.

In drama mode, talk will function in a variety of ways. There will be:

● talk related to the real dimension of the classroom
● 'in role' talk inside the dramatic context which comes out of the experience of interacting in the context and with other role-players
● talk about how to set up the dramatic context and what to use in order to create it
● 'in role' talk inside the dramatic context which also clearly relates back to relationships and needs in the real dimension of the classroom.

Each of these modes of talk will relate to, or be supported by actions and a sense of place, people and experiences. In other words, the talk is about concrete and familiar ideas; it's not abstract, divorced from practicality or obscure in its meanings. Through talk and action of the kind identified above, young people can begin to think about:

- themselves and their relationship to others in the group and to the ideas contained in the drama
- other people's real and 'in role' behaviour and what it says about the context and their involvement with it
- their needs and how to communicate them
- the problem of effectively and realistically re-creating a particular dramatic context
- how the characters in the drama would think, feel and respond to what's going on around them
- any differences between their reaction in role and the way they might respond themselves to similar situations.

If a young person in the dramatic context provided in the 'Disability' example says that, 'No-one is really interested in what I think,' she may be only commenting in role, as the character in the drama, or she may also be echoing her own problem in relating to her classmates in reality. When they in turn advise her on how to get heard, they may also be advising her on her relationship with them! Talk in drama is not real; it is constructed and representative of a particular kind of experience of which the dramatic context that is being worked on is only one example. As in other forms of fiction, there is the opportunity for the context to speak beyond itself – in drama this *actually* happens in participant mode rather than in spectator/observer mode.

If a young person comes to identify with a character or dilemma in drama, she does it by finding an accurate portrayal of the talk and behaviour for her role and her character's reactions to others in the drama. There is an important difference between drama and story here in the sense that it is more difficult to create new personal and social learning through telling stories which are either descriptions of familiar and past events or are heard without the opportunity to go and be inside the story. In drama, the context is built on what is known by the group, but it unfolds as a new story through the spontaneity of the dramatic interactions. At it's most simple it is the difference between, 'That's how it was . . .' and 'This is how it feels . . .'

This dual experiencing of the real world and the imagined

world of the drama provides the opportunity for the teacher to select a dramatic context which serves both to highlight a particular use of talk and which also has the opportunity to respond to students' other needs in the real world. In other words, the teacher may look for a dramatic context which will yield important new learning about language and meanings, and which may also serve as a metaphor for some real individual or group need. As with other forms of fiction in the classroom, the fictional form, itself, is both a passage of communication to the real world of the student and also a form of protection from exposure and insecurity in relation to the real experience of the child.

Many teachers select other kinds of fiction for young people with a similar intent. They consciously attempt to match the child, or group, to a story which may have a special interest or significance. The idea is that the story's ability to speak directly to the child's concerns will encourage the child to discover a new purpose in seeking out and reading/viewing quality fiction. At the same time, teachers recognise that the value of approaching personal and social needs through story is that the child is protected by the world of the fiction from direct exposure or unwarranted probing – the child can choose to identify with the story and seek expression through it, or to take the story as just a story.

It follows that an important difference between participation in dramatic contexts and participation in a real context is that because there are two worlds of talk operating simultaneously – the real dimension of classroom talk and needs, and the imagined talk of the dramatic context – there is a built-in *reflective* dimension to the work. The dramatic context is explicitly negotiated and constructed by those taking part – it's not naturally there, it's *consciously and thoughtfully* brought there through the student's work. This reflective dimension may develop into an unusually high degree of awareness of the student's own thoughts and actions and what these mean in both the real and imagined dimensions. David Booth, a Canadian who has looked closely at both story and drama in young people's lives, makes the point that:

. . . making sense of a story demands that the students apply their own experiences to those in the story. The teacher must constantly help the children go back and forth between their own stories and their own responses, translating the experiences of the story into the context of their own lives. Drama, then, allows the child's own subjective world to come into play, helping them understand the meanings of the story as they live through the drama experience . . . By joining story and drama, children can combine an interest in the lives of story characters with their own struggles for control over their lives. (*Stories in the Classroom*)

The students engaged in both the examples given above are not, therefore, just practising talk in difficult and challenging dramatic contexts. Constructing and reflecting on the dramatic actions and talking are also likely to breed the need in students, who are captured by their engagement in the story, to explore other dimensions of meaning and human experience – the nature of parenting, the nature of disability, moral choices, prejudice etc. both as they affect themselves and also in relation to how they affect others represented by the various roles in the drama.

Through working together to build the drama, students will also have gained insights into each other both through responding to, and reflecting on, the way others have behaved in the drama: the profiles they adopt, their manner of dealing with themselves and others in role etc. All this behaviour speaks of the hopes, fears, attitudes and motives of the real person, not just that of the role that is being adopted.

A particular effect of this reflective quality in drama work will be the ease with which a focus on the development of oracy skills through drama can be married to working in other areas of learning experience, particularly the aesthetic and creative, the personal and social, the spiritual and moral.

The next chapter of this book will go on to consider the use of dramatic contexts as a planning framework for theme and topic based work. It will consider how the features of drama, which have been discussed, so far, in relation to developing language ability and coming to know oneself and the group, can be exploited to enhance a wider range of curriculum purposes.

CHAPTER 3

Drama as a Curriculum Framework

> . . . just as concepts and theory serve to connect the facts of observation and experiment in the conventional disciplines of knowledge, so the great dramatic themes and metaphors provide a basis for organising one's sense of man, for seeing what is persistent in his history and his condition, for introducing *some unity into the scatter of our knowledge as it relates to ourselves.*
> (Jerome Bruner, *Toward a Theory of Instruction*)

The purpose of this chapter is to examine how drama can provide a planning framework for the organisation of a broad range of learning activities in the classroom. The understandings about learning through context developed in Chapter 1 are now applied to the planning of theme and topic work.

Prior to the introduction of the National Curriculum, many primary schools, together with their feeder secondary schools, had already begun to look at ways of providing a bridge between the approach of Key Stage 2 with a generalist class teacher and the subject specialist approach of much secondary schooling. Whilst the National Curriculum has given impetus to further liaison and continuity work between Key Stage 2 and Key Stage 3 this has tended, so far, to focus on record keeping, assessment and professional development. Previously the agenda had tended to be concerned with providing liaison which would offer the child a less threatening and disorientating journey from primary to secondary school and was more concerned with matching teaching styles and learning methods to the child's developmental stage.

One effect of greater dialogue between good primary practice and good secondary practice has been the development of theme and topic work as a means of providing illuminating and meaningful learning connections between different areas of the curriculum (this is most common in Key Stage 2, but it is a form of organisation that is often continued into Years 7/8) and different language tasks (this is most common at Key Stages 3/4, but, increasingly, literature is being used as a thematic base in Key Stages 1/2 as well).

Teachers of English as a subject in Key Stage 3 are now faced with the challenge of resisting the Statutory Orders' preference for splitting literacy back into the discrete components of speaking, listening, reading, writing, spelling, handwriting etc. These teachers are conscious that literacy teaching should seek to integrate language activities so that skills associated with the discrete components are brought together and taught as part of complete and meaningful language activities. In adopting this view literacy teachers are avoiding subscribing to what Frank Smith has called the bureaucratic myth of education:

> The myth is that learning can be guaranteed if instruction is delivered systematically, one piece at a time, with frequent tests to ensure that teachers and students stay on task. (*Insult to Intelligence*)

The problems of overcoming curriculum fragmentation are even more complex for class teachers in Key Stage 2 where efforts to preserve a natural approach to literacy are compounded by the problem of needing to bring coherence and unity to the curriculum as a whole. Class teachers with responsibility for delivering the whole curriculum are acutely aware of the potentially alienating and demoralising effects of presenting young children with an unrecognisable world of learning which has been artificially atomised into discrete targets within individual subjects. The challenge is to find a satisfactory way of organising the curriculum so as to emphasise interrelationships and unities between areas of learning experience. In this way the connections between the experience of learning in the classroom and the child's experience of the world (which is not fragmented but unitary) are strengthened rather than diminished. For such teachers theme and topic work have become routes for accommodating the National Curriculum legislation within an integrated child-centred approach to learning.

Thematic work as a form of curriculum organisation

In suggesting theme and topic work as routes through the problems of curriculum planning, it's important to assert what is meant by these terms and to distinguish between effective and less effective applications of theme and topic planning. For the purposes of this section, therefore, the following limited definition is offered:

Theme is a broad and balanced approach to structuring learning so that a variety of learning activities are drawn together by a common curriculum thread or idea, such as learning relating to 'ourselves', 'flight', 'machines'. A theme achieves breadth and balance when it provides for both affective and cognitive engagement and when the unity of the theme, *from the child's point of view*, is stressed rather than its remaining as a collection of loosely connected classroom activities.

Ironically, thematic organisation has been recently criticised as failing to provide the very coherence it's intended to create:

> The weakest work in primary schools occurs when too many aspects of different subjects are roped together within integrated themes or topic work. There is some good practice but generally topic work is difficult to manage; frequently lacks coherence at the initial planning stage and *consequently is a fragmented experience for the pupils*. ('Standards in Education' *Annual Report of Chief Inspector for Schools 1988–1989*)

It would seem that the actuality of thematic work does not live up to its theoretical potential – why should this be the case?

It is interesting to consider the dominant forms of thematic planning as a way of exploring the gap between the definition of theme offered above and the HMI view that most thematic work does not overcome the problem of curriculum fragmentation for the child. As the report suggests *the problem is often at the initial planning stage*. Figures 9 and 10 attempt to illustrate two conventional approaches to the initial planning of thematic work. The first represents an attempt to relate the theme to the Profile Components and Attainment Targets in the core subjects of the National Curriculum, and the second relates the theme to the areas of learning experience identified as forming the curriculum in *The Curriculum from 5–16*.

Figure 9 clearly illustrates the problem of attempting to make a theme fit the fragmentary nature of the current National Curriculum framework. The diagram only relates relevant aspects of the core subjects and it very quickly becomes an illustration of the danger of attempting to plan when '. . . too many aspects of different subjects are roped together within integrated themes or topic work.' Figure 10 is less fragmentary in the sense that it adopts an approach to planning built round generic areas of experience in which each area subsumes several traditional subject areas.

Science
- types/uses of materials
- forces
- energy
- information technology

English
- speaking and listening
- handwriting

BUILDINGS

Maths
- using/applying maths: problems
- number: operation
- using/applying maths: data/shape
- shape and space: 2D/3D
- shape/space: location/transformations
- handling data

Design & Technology
- appraising
- planning and making
- generating a design proposal
- identifying needs/opportunities

Figure 9 Theme: buildings *related to Profile Components and Attainment Targets*

Humanities
- climate and building design
- buildings through the ages
- disability and building access
- cultural influences on design

Physical
- lifting/carrying
- health & safety
- building physical constructions – pyramids etc.
- pairs and small-group work

Aesthetic & creative
- pictures of our houses/streets
- sketching unusual buildings
- dramas about moving house working in public buildings etc.
- music made from sound collage of building materials/sounds
- dance based on movement of building workers – carrying/lifting etc.

Linguistic & literary
- stories about places we've lived in
- descriptions of ideal homes
- estate agents descriptions
- advertising new homes

Technological
- database for materials and ordering
- use of alternative forms of energy
- CAD
- designing a building

BUILDINGS

Science
- relative tensile strengths of materials
- physical forces in building design
- weathering and erosion
- how building materials are made
- the future – buildings in space

Personal & social
- our homes
- privacy and design
- homes in other lands
- needs of the elderly/disabled etc.

Mathematical
- measurement
- scale drawing
- estimation of materials
- symmetry & geometry in building

Moral & spiritual
- plight of the homeless
- devotional buildings in other cultures
- conservation/environment

Figure 10 Theme: buildings *related to areas of learning experience*

What neither diagram achieves is a child's view of the theme. Both approaches provide the teacher with a useful map of learning, but not in a form that would be recognisable to a child in Key Stages 2/3. If these forms of planning thematic work are dominant in schools, it is not surprising that HMI conclude that they add to, rather than diminish, the fragmented experience of the child.

Both diagrams start from the need to fit curriculum

requirements into a limited amount of space rather than from the child's needs and perspectives. As a result, both fail to provide a recognisable and logical progression for the learner *in the learner's terms*. Moreover, in practice, when following either diagram, it would be easy to slip into the frame of attempting to fit the learners into the curriculum rather than the other way round – which would be to preserve the centrality of the child as in the 'mother-tongue' model (see Figure 2, p. 13).

Ultimately, the teacher is not helped by such diagrams because they give no indication of the *process* of the theme. In other words, what will guide the movement from one form of learning experience to another? Surely not the timetable alone! What are the stages of the theme's management which ensure that the theme develops in depth of learning and challenges for the learner? What is the logic of the theme from the child's point of view – what will their map look like?

A child-centred approach to theme planning

If curriculum planning begins with establishing how the child will view the theme *before* it goes on to map out the learning potential through reference to Attainment Targets or discrete areas of educational experience, then the problems of fragmentation and sequencing learning effectively begin to pale. In planning terms, a child-centred approach will be influenced by the desire to re-create the circumstances and structures of mother-tongue learning in the design and implementation of the theme. These may be briefly stated as:

- *a reliance on story* as the principle means of storing and interrogating meanings and experiences
- the importance of *first hand, practical experience*; the desire on the teacher's part to show children the theme in an authentic context rather than tell about it out of context
- the need to let children *invent problems* and their solutions
- the importance of *purposeful talk*, collaboration, social interaction and affective involvement in mother-tongue learning approaches
- the importance of *connecting the teaching of ideas and skills to real human activity*

- the need for the teacher to *contextualise* skills, attitudes, concepts and knowledge within recognisable human situations in which people need particular skills etc. in order to overcome problems or to develop towards a desired goal.

Figure 11 attempts to set out the planning of the same building theme within a child-centred view. The plan operates on a dual path. One path maps out the actions associated with actually building a building; the other is an educational path that focusses on human issues stemming from the theme: research opportunities connected with the actions, assessment tasks woven into the actions and a checklist of the Skills, Attitudes, Concepts and Knowledge (S.A.C.K.) demanded by the actions. By inviting the children to engage with the theme, *in role*, as 'builders' faced with the challenge of making a building together, the theme becomes recognisable to everyone as a job in the real world that needs doing.

ACTIONS IN THE DRAMA	Human Issues	Research Opportunities	Assessment Tasks	S.A.C.K.
● Select suitable site	● Concern for local environment	● What makes a piece of land suitable for building?		e.g.
● Decide on type of building	● Needs of old people	● What are the special needs of elderly people?		● Organisation
● Select tools and trades	● Relationships between workers	● What are the different skills required for building? What do different tools do? How does a building start?		● Problem solving
● Prepare site	● Team work			● Health/Safety
● Mark out and measure site	● Discovery of historical artefacts	● What is the sequence of work?		● Measurement
● Dig footings	● Health & Safety	● How has the land been used in the past?		● Estimation
● Order materials	● Looking after previous occupant of the site	● What are the dangers involved & how can builders protect themselves?		● Selection of tools and materials
● Mix cement	● Ensuring building responds to needs .	● What happens to displaced people?		● Continuity of time and place
● Build walls etc.	● Helping elderly make a home for themselves in new building	● How is cement made? How are bricks laid? How are materials estimated?		● Relationships at work
		● How are buildings insulated? How can buildings be adapted to occupants' needs?		● Co-ordination
				● Precision
				● Relative strengths of materials
				● Role models
				● Quantity/Quality
				● Crafting
				● Tool use

Figure 11 Theme: building and builders
Human context – Working as builders on a community housing project

The problems of sequencing learning activities is largely overcome, in Figure 11, by allowing the class to follow the *natural* sequence of events in building a building. The management of the theme will depend on the teacher's willingness to move the class from working in drama – 'as if' they were authentically constructing a building – to research in the classroom designed to enable learning the necessary skills, concepts and understanding required to complete a building.

For younger students the drama will be physical, busy and concentrate on social interaction, problem invention and solution and teamwork. For older students there will be greater emphasis on the responsibilities and competencies of their roles as architects, planners, builders' merchants etc. There may also be an emphasis on a particular aspect of the work, developing data bases and spreadsheets for the project or focussing on the different registers and uses of language available in the context. The classroom work may resemble conventional learning activity, but, in the drama, the talk will resonate with the everyday discourse of workers dealing with problems, the need to progress with the imagined building project and concern for the needs of the people who will be housed in the building and the people living nearby.

In order to do the job authentically, the children will need to pause regularly and discover what skills and concepts are required in order to move on with the job. Because the plan follows an authentic model from life, it will inevitably offer natural opportunities for a broad and balanced learning menu which will encompass not only the core and foundation subjects but cross-curricular themes as well. This effect of using drama to re-create 'real life' demands and situations for the learner not only provides relevance but also coherence to the curriculum. It is also worth noting that the 'realness' of learning through dramatic context also encompasses 'real world' pressures like deadlines, difficult work forces, conflicts between economic and human needs and bad weather!

This 'drama context' approach is particularly valuable in themes or topics which relate to communities or occupations, when children can engage with the theme by being shown in context what it is like to work as people in the real or historical world rather than merely learning about them through being told out of context.

However, it will not always be appropriate for a teacher to consider framing an entire theme within a single dramatic context in this way. In this case the teacher may be interested in introducing a drama as part of the theme as a way of:

- **Applying skills, concepts, attitudes and knowledge to 'real life' situations**

  An elderly shopkeeper receives a formal letter from a

property developer, who is also the leaseholder, which informs him that the corner shop will be demolished to make way for a new precinct. The class are in role as customers asked by the shopkeeper for help – the developer refuses to attend any meetings and insists that any appeal is made in writing and must put forward the case for the shop being more important than the new precinct. In order to help the shopkeeper, the class must:

- read the developer's letter
- understand basic property law
- interview local people
- frame questionnaires
- rally support
- frame the letter in response with due regard to register, audience and intention.

● **Providing aesthetic and creative experiences**
In order to create the human context, the class engage in a range of creative activities designed to create concern and interest in the shopkeeper's dilemma and to bring balance to the theme:

- space in the classroom is arranged to represent the shop. What does it sell? What does it look and smell like? What objects in the shop symbolise the memories of the old person? How does the shopkeeper look after reading the letter?
- the class use movement to create a dream sequence of memories as the shopkeeper sits and remembers the past. Through dance they create images of childhood, family, war, change.

● **Motivating writing and talk**
In addition to the letter to the developer, the class also contribute writing in the form of old letters kept by the shopkeeper, diary entries to go with the memories, petitions and newspaper articles, poems capturing the atmosphere of the shop.

The talk demands include: interviewing customers, holding meetings and a difficult scene where the old person barricades himself in the shop with a gun kept from the war for security purposes – the class have to find a way of talking the shopkeeper out of harming himself or others.

- **Challenging or developing attitudes and values**
  Through the careful selection of her own roles, the teacher is able to challenge and develop the class' understanding through her interactions in role.

  The shopkeeper is not a sympathetic figure: he is intolerant of children and (although himself an immigrant) of new immigrants and fairly brusque with his customers. Why should anyone want to help him?

  The developer is apparently a warm and concerned individual who believes that the precinct will better serve the needs of the community, particularly children and young mothers, although the plans reveal an inaccessible, concrete wasteland designed to accommodate the cars of out-of-town shoppers and to exploit the spending power of the young.

- **Creating interest in remote and unfamiliar areas of learning**
  The context has generated an interest in a range of human issues to do with age, prejudice, ambition, community needs, progress. It has also touched on legal concepts and generated a range of writing tasks in which the needs of the context have led to particular attention being paid to technical accuracy, register, layout etc.

- **Providing a narrative or metaphor as a 'holding form' for skills etc.**
  The connecting thread that binds the various learning areas and tasks which have been described in this example has been the story of the old shopkeeper. Each of the learning tasks has resulted from some need in the story which the class have wanted to respond to. The completion of these tasks have in turn had practical effects on the story's development, so that the class have been helped to see: the logic and sequence of the activities and tasks they have been involved in; the connections between learning tasks and 'real life' situations; how skills gained in the classroom will have powerful effects in later life.

▬ Drama as part of an environmental theme in ▬ (Key Stages 2/3)

. . . drama can play an important part in developing aesthetic appreciation of the environment. [It] offers the opportunity to understand the aesthetic aspects of the environment and the conflicts which can arise between aesthetic, utilitarian and economic considerations (*Curriculum Guidance 7*)

The class had begun work by looking at their immediate home and school environments in terms of the human influences: obvious abuses of the environment; projects for reducing pollution, recycling and renewing waste materials; differences between organic and non-organic waste materials.

The work was now moving on to consider pollution on a wider scale in terms of the damage to the ozone layer, destruction of natural habitats and air-borne pollutants. The class began to lose confidence in the project as it moved away from the familiarity of their home environments. The teacher introduced a poem by the Canadian poet Sean O'Huigin as a starting point for drama. The poem provides a metaphor for the effects of pollution through the idea of a fearsome dragon trapped beneath the ice, the ice is slowly melting causing the release of the dragon to cause havoc:

> . . . beneath the drifts
> of glittering snow
> lies something evil
> something low
> something with long icy teeth
> something curled up
> underneath the
> ancient glaciers'
> mighty cliffs
> with blue cold steely
> snarling lips
> for centuries
> it's lain there
> trapped inside
> its icy lair
> listening as
> each year goes
> past to the
> winter's icy
> blast
> but bit by bit
> and drop by drop
> as humans make the
> air grow hot
> pumping garbage
> and pollution
> they give to it a
> neat solution to its

problem of
entrapment
it grinds its jaws
it tries to snap
them

(extract from *Atmosfear*)

- The drama starts with the teacher explaining that the class will be working 'in role' as scientists working at a secret research station somewhere in England. Their job is to conduct experiments into changes in the environment. (Up until this point in the theme the class had indeed been working with scientific methodology in order to collect, store and handle data from their own local research projects; they were, therefore, becoming familiar with research methods and the use of information technology in this area of inquiry.)

- The class form themselves into groups and are asked to decide on a particular experiment they might be concerned with in their role as a team of 'scientists'; they are encouraged to consider the 'big' problems that affect the environment and which receive regular media attention.

- Having decided on what aspect of the environment they were interested in, the groups freely play at being scientists involved in experiments at the centre. The teacher goes into groups in role as the Centre Administrator to ask how the work is going, to suggest ideas, to ask about resource requirements and to hold meetings where the scientists can discuss the progress of their work and its implications for the world. During periods of reflection, the group compare their 'play' experiments with actual meteorological and climatic experiments being undertaken in the world.

- Once the teacher feels that the class are involved and interested in their new roles, she calls a meeting and informs the scientists that there is a visitor who has been brought to the centre because she has a special problem which they might be able to help with. The class are asked to prepare themselves for the visitor who is nervous and unsure of the scientists.

- The teacher returns to the meeting in the role of an Innuit woman who has travelled to seek help from the peoples of the south. The teacher continues to develop the role, sometimes in response to questions from the scientists, sometimes in order to prompt further questions. She tells her story – she lives by the lake of diamonds a beautiful expanse of ice which sparkles in the sun. One day, not so long ago, she was walking on the ice when she noticed a huge crack which had never been there before. She bent down to look more closely at it and then she heard a terrible sound, she was scared, but as she listened she recognised words which in the scientists' language meant:

"When the ashes fall from the south, and the snow turns to stinging rain, then the dragons will fly again . . ."

- The Innuit woman says that she knows the scientists probably have not time for her stories, but there are legends amongst her people which speak of a time when great beasts strode the world and that the ice came and covered them. Now she notices that the ice is getting thinner. The voice warned of a threat from the south so she is asking the scientists whether the story has any meaning for them and whether they might come to the north to investigate her story.

- The scientists show the Innuit woman around the centre explaining their experiments. Then they work on compiling an inventory of clothing and special equipment needed to undertake the journey to the frozen north.

- The drama continues as an adventure in which the scientists travel by plane, learn to drive dog teams and sledges, meet other Innuit, go to the lake and carry out experiments and send a message to the governments of the world warning of the danger.

A child-centred approach to theme planning (Key Stage 3)

Opportunities for cross-curricular links at Key Stage 3 are often limited by the institutional constraints of timetabling and staffing. In some cases, however, a measure of integration between English, Drama and Humanities may be preserved in Years 6–8. The National Curriculum framework does give specialist teachers an insight into the content and sequence of learning in other areas which in turn provides the chance for collaborative planning of theme work in which a number of specialist concerns can be included within a thematic approach.

The idea of collaboration between specialists in order to teach thematically may also provide a means of rationalising an overcrowded subject-driven timetable and of preserving coherence and continuity for the child.

The following example is offered as an approach to thematic teaching in Year 7 which preserves the features of mother-tongue learning identified earlier in this chapter. The example brings together the aesthetic/creative, linguistic/literary and historical areas of learning experience. The motive for the project was to find a teaching approach to the Peasant's Revolt of 1381 which would allow the class access to the major themes of the subject without their being swamped by data relating to the period.

━━━ Example: The Peasant's Revolt ━━━ (Key Stage 3)

- The teacher introduces the theme by offering the class pictures and images of the time and asking them to look for evidence of housing, work, food, clothing, beliefs. A short synopsis of the period immediately before the Revolt is given – feudalism, the Black Death, war with France.

- The class are given an authentic speech made by the Hedge-Priest John Ball:

> "My friends, our lives are poor and miserable. Things are wrong with England and they will not be put right unless we do something about them. Poor man hates rich man; rich man sets his face against poor man. Nothing will be better until the good things are shared out fairly.
>
> The rich man wears beautiful clothes and eats fine food from silver plates. We wear coarse cloth and eat dry bread from a wooden platter. He drinks wine, we have nothing but water. He sleeps in a bed between linen sheets; we have to put up with mouldy straw on the ground.
>
> What makes him think he is better than us? We are all children of Adam and Eve. How did he get rich at our expense?"

In groups, the class are set the task of using the speech in a number of contrasting social contexts, in order to explore how the delivery and impact of the speech might change according to a given context. *This form of work is familiar as a result of work in English on the relationship between talk, audience and context.*

The contexts are:

- a speech delivered in a peasant's house to persuade a family to join the revolt (the family are split over the issue)
- a speech delivered at a large gathering of peasants
- a speech delivered at a large gathering of peasants with soliders present who have been ordered to arrest John Ball if he stirs up trouble
- a speech delivered to fellow prisoners in Maidstone Gaol with guards outside the door.

- Each group selects at least two contexts to work with and act out. They are only able to use the words of the speech, but they are encouraged to use as much non-verbal signing as will be necessary to convey accurately the sense of chosen context. *The group are familiar with this approach from their work in Drama which has taught them how gesture, spatial relationships, tension and atmosphere can be used to convey meanings.*

- The class use their knowledge of human behaviour to create apparently unfamiliar and distant contexts. They are able to draw on their understanding of the likely interpersonal tensions in each context in order to portray the different effects of speech. Constructing the contexts requires further research and the lesson serves to encourage interest in further study of the period.

- The class move on to consider the nature of feudalism and they work in groups on using drama and movement to make an animated model of a feudal society based on the conventional pyramid illustration found in many history books. The technical problems of re-creating the pyramid and its power relationships using others in the class generates talk and questions about the nature and equity of feudalism.

CHAPTER 4

Managing and Planning Drama in Key Stages 2/3

Managing learning from within the drama

The process of learning through being involved in dramatic contexts may be greatly enhanced by the teacher entering into the improvisation and interacting with the young people involved in order to stir up and disturb expectations or stale views and pinpoint aspects of the situation which the students may not yet have considered. This involves teaching as part of the context. In other words, the teacher works in role, inside the context, using her own communications in the symbolic dimension ('make believe') of the drama in order to assist teaching which will enter into the real dimension of children's learning about language.

The teacher who works inside the improvisation is able to bring her skills of management and story, together with her understanding of the class and its needs, to the art form of drama in order to help students achieve more through their involvement than might otherwise have been the case if they had been left to introduce these important elements of their own accord. *It is of course important to remember that the teacher is entering the students' improvisation on very special terms.* Teachers in Key Stage 1, and others who are close to children when imaginative play is still very prevalent in their behaviour, will tell you that children will quickly reject adult involvement in play which is proprietary, or is patronising and belittling. The teacher enters into role in order to enhance that experience for the students, to bring strategies and skills which will help the students towards self-discovery through their own experience of the improvisation as well as to provide the opportunity for reflection on it.

Working in role provides a very different medium for teaching about talk. The teacher is able to model and demonstrate register, tone, purpose and contextual awareness through her own interactions with fellow participants in the drama. *The teacher, crucially, is able to operate 'in role' relationships, and therefore introduce new language possibilities, that would not otherwise be possible* (see Figure 5, p. 22 and the model of mother-tongue learning, p. 13). She is able, for instance, to enter into the improvisation as someone needing help, as someone who genuinely doesn't know answers, as someone of a different age, race, class, ability, gender, as someone approaching authority, as someone dealing with a disability. Each one of these roles creates new and interesting talk demands for students that would not be possible to experience by any other means of teaching.

If the students are willing to accept the teacher into their improvisation then they will also be willing to suspend their disbelief about the teacher's actual role. This feature of involvement in fiction – we work as if it's real, even though we are clear it is not – provides the kind of learning which occurs in life, often painfully. We learn about context from encountering it daily in our lives. *But* we can also learn about it indirectly and safely through improvising 'life' in dramatic contexts.

In drama, the teacher is also offering the protection that comes because the activity is not real, so 'mistakes' may be made, challenges may be offered without the resultant consequences that would happen in life. The 'make believe' of fictional form provides some distance for the students from their own, possibly painful, immediate experience and identity.

By carefully constructing the context for an improvisation and by working in role, the teacher is able to demonstrate actively the effect of context on talk and then help students to reflect on the experience so that there is a movement from action and talk embedded in a specific context towards generalisations about the effect of social context on human relationships. By working in role the teacher is able:

- **to define the available space**, e.g. work with the different effects of proximity and distance between talkers, use furniture to explore status relationships – sitting behind a desk as a boss, for example, or the difference between operating in one's own territory or home as opposed to being confronted in official or alien spaces
- **to model different uses of register, tone and vocabulary** and in so doing encourage young people to try out unfamiliar registers or forms of language
- **to respond authentically to student behaviour which breaks the**

dominant social code, e.g. 'I will not be shouted at, you've had your chance and now I'm not staying to hear any more', or, 'I had hoped to get a fair hearing but I see now that this is all a huge joke for you!'

- **to reference significant aspects of the context in a reflective way**, e.g. 'Perhaps she'd have told us more if we had chosen somewhere less threatening to hold this meeting', or, 'When we get to the factory owner's house, shall we knock at the front door, or go round to the kitchen as we have been told to?'

- **to challenge stereotypic expectations of the context**, e.g. 'You seem surprised by my refusal. Did you assume I would give in to your wishes simply because I am a woman?', or 'Why do you assume that because we have not progressed in your western terms, we have not progressed as a people?'

- **to encourage and support participation in the improvisation**, e.g. 'If you have something on your mind this is your chance, I won't let them hurt you', or, 'There are voices here which are not getting a fair hearing, why don't you listen again to what has just been said?'

Whilst the idea of working inside the improvisation is recognised by many teachers as offering great potential for learning, many teachers also remain anxious about the apparent difficulties involved. There is always going to be challenge and risk involved in teaching in role, but these risks and challenges may now seem more welcome in the era of a National Curriculum when so much has been made predictable and is determined by external agencies, so that the space for teachers to explore and use their professional instincts has been greatly reduced. There are, however, a number of strategies and understandings available to teachers which can reduce the risks and complexities of management to acceptable levels.

Creating a climate in which drama is valued by the staff as a whole
A professional climate is needed in which individual teachers are not censured for taking professional risks and talking through difficulties encountered in the classroom. *Aspects of Primary Education: Drama* identifies the following relevant characteristics of good practice:

- a commitment from the head teacher and staff that children should be involved in active learning

- an enthusiasm for drama amongst staff
- a secure place for drama within programme planning
- a tradition of drama within the school exists and there is an expectation that drama will be accorded its due respect and value, part of which lies in the enjoyment and strong sense of commitment which it generates amongst children.

Some teachers may be fortunate enough to work in environments which already reflect these characteristics. Others may need to work towards establishing the characteristics through dialogue with senior management, governors and other staff; sharing teaching; providing resources and ideas for others to use; insisting on training for drama as a statutory element in the National Curriculum; making contact with local advisers and others.

Choosing the physical space used for drama carefully
The risk of losing control of a group is greatly reduced through the careful selection of space and time. If there is the opportunity to be flexible about the space used for drama, then it is better to opt for spaces which children associate with calm, reflective activity rather than choosing spaces which children associate with highly active, physical activity. If a group changes into P.E. kit and goes into the hall for drama, they are bound to have an expectation that the drama will allow them to run around in a big empty space! On the other hand, if the teacher uses the carpet, or story area in a Key Stage 2 classroom, or the English classroom in Key Stage 3, then the children will expect the activity to be controlled, reflective and to involve careful listening as well as talk. Large spaces do offer great potential in drama, but a teacher may want to be confident about controlling drama in more intimate and familiar spaces before moving into large open areas.

Negotiating the ground rules for interpersonal behaviour
The students are also being asked to accept risk and challenge in drama, so it makes sense for both the teacher and the students to have the protection of negotiated and publicly displayed ground rules which will serve as pre-requisites for the activity. These ground rules may cover areas such as:

- interruptions – the right to speak and be heard
- physical behaviour – limits on the space, unacceptable physicality, pushing, punching etc.

- the right not to take a role
- unacceptable challenges to the teacher's authority whilst in role, or to other children in role
- the level of seriousness and attentiveness required
- a willingness to suspend individual needs in favour of responding to the needs of a group as a whole.

Introducing the convention of the teacher working in role
Before engaging in a sustained improvisation, the teacher may want to get students used to the idea of the teacher working from within a fiction. In Key Stage 2 this is easily done as part of sharing stories with children where the teacher, working in the story-corner of a classroom, can offer to answer questions about the story as one of the characters involved. This questioning may only last a few minutes and be seen as an additional extension of discussion and active comprehension. In Key Stage 3 the teacher may want to distance this questioning, e.g. 'If I was Julie's best friend, I would say to her . . . How do you think Julie might respond to that? . . . O.K. Well, does someone want to speak as Julie and I will answer as the friend? . . . Then we can all have a go working in pairs.' In this way, the convention of the teacher working in role can be introduced in a secure and systematic fashion.

Sharing responsibility for the quality and direction of the drama
It has been a continual theme in this book that young people are particularly experienced in story and imaginative play from their own cultural experience and from their dependence on fiction as a means of exploring and confirming reality. Young people also gain understanding of what makes a good fiction from their continual exposure to stories, TV, film etc. The teacher does not need to feel burdened with the development of a drama or to feel the pressure of 'thinking on the hoof'. The students will be able to make useful suggestions about ways of developing the drama and ways of intensifying the atmosphere and tension. As students learn more about the available forms and conventions in drama, they will also make constructive proposals about how the development of the drama might be handled.

Interspersing dramatic activity with other ways of working
Sustaining drama over long periods requires considerable experience for students and teachers alike. Where the dramatic activity is closely related to on-going classroom work it becomes

possible to move from drama to other work which is motivated by and related to the drama, and which will, therefore help in the development of the dramatic context, e.g. writing, further reading, illustrations, design, problem solving and research etc. (See examples of 'Supporting techniques and strategies' that follow.) Breaking the drama down to manageable and short intervals provides a breathing space for reflection and collecting feedback on progress and possible developments.

Working with smaller groups
There is no reason why the teacher needs to work in role with the whole class at one time, indeed as class sizes continue to grow as a result of cutbacks in spending, it becomes increasingly difficult to attempt the idea of whole-class improvisations. Observing the spontaneous improvising of others is a legitimate form of learning in its own right, so it makes sense for the teacher to consider working in role with a few students at a time whilst inviting others to become involved – through discussion or through substitution – with those participating in the improvisation. Two strategies are particularly useful in this respect: '**Forum theatre**' (see Supporting techniques and strategies **14**, p. 57) and '**Multiple contexts**' (see Supporting techniques and strategies **27**, p. 60).

▬ *Supporting techniques and strategies* ▬

Drama provides a rich variety of conventions and techniques other than spontaneous improvisation involving the teacher. There is an assumption in this chapter that improvisation of this kind is particularly powerful in terms of language development but the following list is provided to bring variety to drama work (these techniques may or may not involve the teacher directly):

- 1 to 5 are of particular value in building understanding of the story used for drama or the story of the drama itself
- 6 to 11 allow for the recording or physical representation of the context of the story or the context of the drama
- 12 to 27 provide a way of assisting or interrupting improvisation.

1 Telling a story from different points of view
In pairs or groups, the story is retold in the voice of characters other than the narrator so as to see how it might change

according to viewpoint. One member of the group starts the retelling then passes it on to the next at a given signal; a signal is also given to change the voice of the storyteller – this game is a fun way of exploring voice in story.

2 Pairs of characters talking about incidents from the story
Pairs take on the roles of people in the story, or people affected by the story, and talk about the events of the story in the form of gossip, rumour and speculations.

3 People outside the story commenting on the characters and events
Pairs or groups improvise formal or informal situations as teachers, neighbours, social workers, relatives etc.

4 Scenes representing group prediction of the next part of the story
At key moments, a story – which is being read or told – is stopped, and groups are invited to prepare improvisations, or to set up a spontaneous improvisation, exploring where the story might go next.

5 Telephone conversations between characters
Working in pairs, one character communicates news or developments to the other character, who will be affected by the news in some way, or, one character rings a group of other characters, so that as well as the telephone conversation there is also talk amongst the group about what to say or do.

6 Letters, diaries or notes written by, or between, characters
These can be introduced as a stimulus to the improvisations, e.g. 'We've just received this telegram, it's for you . . .' or written in response to events, feelings, thoughts generated by the improvisation, e.g. 'What would X have written in her diary that night?'

7 Props or important objects drawn or made by the class
These may be used in the improvisation, or used as an aid to reflection, e.g. 'Now X is grown up she holds the picture taken that day when she was a child, what does she say as she looks at it now, what memories does it hold for her?'

8 Designing or drawing costumes

These can be used as a way of building belief in another historical/cultural setting, or as a way of clarifying detail, e.g. 'How easy would it be for a Victorian woman to move freely and be active? What do the clothes tell us about Victorian lifestyle and values?'

9 Rearranging the classroom to represent an important 'space'

This could be a room, a cabin, market place, shop floor or some other environment described in the story or which will form the physical context for improvisation. This is a very useful means of establishing belief; building character through consideration of how a living/working space might be furnished by the character/s; providing a limited and controlled space for improvisation. It may be 'built' using available furniture and objects as 'props', or a group may visualise what they imagine to be in a defined empty space as they look at it. In dramas which involve small groups going back to bases – homes, departments, sections etc. – mats or chairs may be used to mark out the parameters of the bases.

10 Compiling oral reports, dossiers, or secret files kept by security forces etc.

These records may be used as basis for interviewing/ interrogating characters as suspects or as witnesses, or they may be used in courtroom and inquest scenes. Groups may prepare improvisations showing how the information has been gathered, or they may have to present evidence to a superior as a briefing.

11 Outline of a character

A large outline of a figure is put on the wall so that the group can fill in thoughts, feelings, observations and things said or done by a character. The outline can be added to over time so that it becomes an accumulative record during the reading of the story of how the character is built up. In improvisation, the outline can be used as an aid to reflection and to check that action and talk is true to character.

12 Hot-seating characters about their motives and reactions

One or more characters allow themselves to be formally questioned by the rest of the group who may speak as themselves or in role as other characters or media representatives etc. The questioning may reveal motives, reactions to events, contradictory accounts of the same event, pleas for help and assistance or the teacher may take a role and be hot-seated in order to pass on specialist information which the group needs, or to develop the tension in the story or to deepen thinking in the group.

13 Alternative scenes involving the characters
These could be the improvisation of scenes not covered in the story or parallel scenes which would throw more light on the characters; the scenes may be an attempt to re-create events before or after the events in the story or drama.

14 Forum-theatre
This is a very useful form of spontaneous improvisation in which a small group acts out a scene watched by the rest of the class. The actors and the audience are able to stop the action to ask for advice, to check the truthfulness of the role-playing, monitor shifts in attitude and changes in understanding caused by the improvisation. Students in the audience can change places with role-players in order to demonstrate a different way of playing the role or to suggest a strategy for overcoming a problem faced by one of the characters in the improvisation.

15 Teacher/leader in role as a starting point
As for **12**, but used as a way of introducing a story or dramatic context, e.g. 'Let's start off by talking to someone who has a story to tell/knows more about the events we are interested in . . .' or, the teacher is modelled into a statue of the character by the class; this may include working on a character's movement and way of talking.

16 Meeting of characters
A public meeting is held between the characters chaired by the teacher or a member of the class, e.g. villagers attending a parish council meeting etc. As for **3** and **13**, but spontaneously improvised as a means of: moving the story on; sharing and solving a problem; negotiating a collective action or highlighting conflicting points of view.

17 Still images representing 'illustrations' of key events
This is a very economical and controlled way of working in which groups use themselves to make pictures, or statues, which represent key moments, ideas, relationships etc. They may be in the form of posters, photographs, paintings, illustrations in a

book, civic memorials, tapestries, murals etc. They can be used as a way of starting, e.g. 'Make an image which shows us something about the way we treat the environment'; as a way of reflecting on the improvisation, e.g. 'As the two sides face each other across the disputed territory, what image does each have of the future?'; or as a way of reviewing the meaning of an improvisation, e.g. 'If the people living in this street were to commission a mural to remind them of these events, what form would it take? What would be in it?'

18 The media perspective on characters and events from the story

As for 2, 3 and 10 but from the perspective of the media. What would be newsworthy? How would the media respond to these events? There is an opportunity for 'outside' broadcasts, news stories, 'chat show' interviews and still images of events and roles already in the drama to add depth to the improvisation and heighten tensions.

19 Family, or group, photographs

As in 17, groups use themselves to make pictures, a useful means of exploring public and private worlds: images are made to contrast the formal picture that is publicly displayed against the more private, intimate picture kept secretly out of view.

20 Still image representing a character's image of past or future events

As in 17, as a means of building a sense of how a character's present action may have been formed by events in the past, or by hopes and fears of the future, e.g. 'When Rosa Parks refused to give up her seat to a white man that day in Montgomery, Alabama, what might she have been thinking of in the past of her people, or in her dream of the future?'

21 The 'freeze-frame' as a way of holding the action

Students' familiarity with video recorders allows them the facility to freeze the action of an improvisation, perhaps because things are moving too quickly, because there is an opportunity for reflection on what's going on, or because the teacher sees a piece of quality work beginning to degenerate! Once stopped, the action and position of the characters can be read and commented on. Freeze-framing may also be used to start an improvisation, e.g. 'In your roles, go and join the people waiting for news at the pithead, find a position which shows us your concern and then freeze. When the picture is complete the manager will come forward and start the improvisation.'

22 Making a sound collage to accompany action
This can be used as a way of building belief and creating atmosphere, e.g. 'Let's create the sounds of the woods that night' or 'As Jack walked towards the market place, what familiar sounds did he hear?'

23 Mimed actions with an accompanying narration by the teacher
The teacher takes the role of a narrator whilst the students continue action without speech in order to move time on, e.g. 'The days passed until eventually the day came when the fields were ready for the seed to be planted'; or to control the action, e.g. 'The searchers moved very slowly and quietly towards the deserted hut, they stopped and paused to listen five feet from its door'; or to provide tension and atmosphere, e.g. 'She sat listening, not daring to make a sound, an open magazine lay on her knee, the coffee beside her was cold – then she heard the familiar faltering steps on the stairs.'

24 Hearing the thinking of characters at key moments
Students have the opportunity to express the interior speech of their role, which will provide a different view of the action, deepen response and contrast what is said with what is meant. Language and register may be modelled by the teacher, e.g. 'As I stand now as an old woman, thoughts of how it used to be flood my mind, and I find myself thinking . . .'; or one group may provide the thoughts for another group's actions, or figures in a still image might be asked for their thoughts as a way of explaining their image.

25 Voices of indecision heard at key moments of choice in the improvisation
Where a character in the story is faced with a difficult decision or a difficult task, the rest of the group form a tunnel for the character to pass through on their way to the place where the decision must be taken. Voices in the tunnel offer advice, warnings, quotes from things said earlier in the drama – at the end of the tunnel the character decides what to do.

26 A character is played collectively

This is a means of allowing students to collaborate in the expression of a role which is of particular interest or importance. There may be several characters involved, each represented by a small group of students or the whole class, who can all speak as the character, e.g. the teacher enters a circle as a girl late home, the class ask her questions in the collective role of her brother lying awake waiting for her; or a confrontation between two characters is played out by two groups representing the characters and each side takes it in turn to add to their character's arguments or to respond to counter-arguments from the other side.

27 A character moves from one social context to another

The effect of the multiple contexts is to show different facets of the character's personality. Small groups prepare contexts for improvisation based on key events or encounters in the character's life; the teacher (in role as the character) goes from group to group improvising the character's responses to the context. What picture of the character is built up through the various improvisations (for example, a homeless teenager is seen through the contexts of the last meal at home, with friends at a club, last contact with school, negotiating a place in a squat, dealing with the police)?

For a more comprehensive listing of techniques and their applications see:

Making Sense of Drama (Heinemann, 1984),
Structuring Drama Work (Cambridge University Press, 1990),
Jonothan Neelands.
'Appendix six', *English 5–16 Consultation Document* (NCC).

▬ *A framework for planning drama* ▬

This chapter has concentrated so far on the difficult business of managing and developing drama. This management will need to go on within some sort of framework for the drama which will help the teacher keep in mind the aims of the teaching and the needs of her class. Figure 12 outlines a planning process which may assist teachers in mapping out their thinking in preparation for drama – it also serves to review the key understandings and perspectives on drama offered throughout this book:

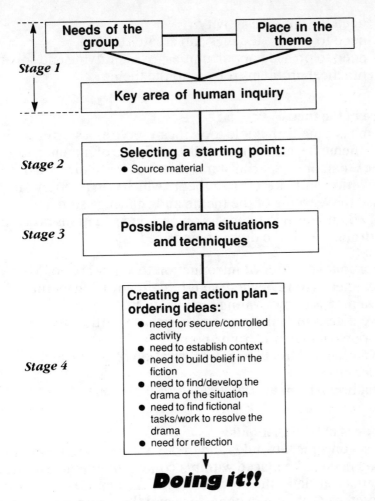

Figure 12 A planning process for drama

━━━ Stage 1   Clarifying aims and objectives ━━━

Initial thinking about the drama will be influenced by three sets of concerns:

● **Needs of the group**
What does the drama need to address in the group and in the individuals within it?

- need for greater co-operation
- need to clarify and make concrete an abstract or obscure meaning
- need to build self-confidence and esteem

— 61 —

- need for physical activity
- need to engage feelings and create concern
- need to provide opportunities for identifying and solving practical problems related to the theme.

● **Place in the theme**

Drama is a highly flexible tool: it can serve as a starting point for a theme because it relies on knowledge of human nature rather than upon specialist information; it can provide fresh motivation and interest to a theme which is in mid-flow; it can utilise the learning of the theme and challenge students to apply their learning to new problems and situations posed in the drama; so, is the drama being used as:

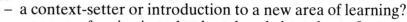

- a context-setter or introduction to a new area of learning?
- a means of reviewing what has already been learnt?
- a means of motivating further study?
- a means of making or emphasising a particular perspective or learning point?
- a practical 'real life' demonstration of an abstract concept?
- a break from analytic/scientific approaches?

● **Key area of human inquiry**

Skills, concepts, attitudes and understandings relating to the theme need to be placed within a context of human experience – drama translates the abstract world back into the concreteness of human behaviour and then, through reflection, returns to a consideration of abstract ideas. In this sense, dramas stand as human examples of abstract ideas and skills.

As students being to explore the sub-text of the story, they move from an enactment of literal information into an exploration of the concepts that lie under the plot skeleton. (David Booth, *Stories in the Classroom*)

- What will the drama set out to explore or question?
- What is the 'real-life' importance of the theme?
- What aspect of human experience will the theme focus on?
- Can the title of the theme or topic be re-stated as a question about human experience?

Stage 2   Selecting a starting point

For teachers of literacy, starting points for drama will be found in fiction. A story or poem provides the teacher and the group with a fictional 'for instance' of the theme, complete with a narrative, characters, descriptions of place and time, affective response and the aesthetic of the storyteller/poet. Stories will suggest scenes, encounters, dilemmas, choices, struggles, failures and celebrations which can then form the basis for drama work, which is not to suggest, of course, that drama is simply retelling the existing plot or repeating what is already known in the story.

The starting point for the drama needs to be rooted in human experience. The experience itself may be real to the individuals involved in the activity or it may be imagined, reported, or historical. In addition to stories and poems, there are many other starting points which may include:

- concept such as 'freedom'
- newspaper account
- photograph or painting
- play script
- primary or secondary historical source
- facsimile documents
- an image or sculpture
- an object associated with the experience
- map or diagram
- music and sounds
- lyrics
- an expression of feeling within the group.

The starting point should be selected according to its capacity to bring an otherwise abstract theme into the intellectual and emotional comprehension of the students (helping the group to make human contact with the theme), so that responses and questions can be shared and some element of the theme can be located within their own personal and collective experience. Some experiences, or concepts associated with the theme, may be so far removed, or so abstract, that a source is required which makes the experience manageable for participants. The biblical story of Solomon may serve as a source for an exploration of concepts of justice and fairness; the story of a building being constructed may serve as a source for an exploration of the concepts of measurement, estimation and formula.

The teacher must search for a possible starting point that is relevant to the child's experience, relevant to the spirit of the story, and a vehicle for confrontation through language (Connie and Harold Rosen, *The Language of Primary School Children*.)

For the dramatic activity to be worthwhile, the source needs to find a response in those taking part. The selection and introduction of a particular source as an appropriate starting point for dramatic activity is clearly a crucial matter. It may be influenced by criteria such as the source's potential:

- to translate accurately a human experience into terms which can be recognised and understood by the students
- to represent the experience in an accessible combination of words, images and feelings
- to capture immediately the interest and imagination of a group
- to give sufficient information about an experience and to engage feelings
- to speak directly to the group's current preoccupations
- to motivate a desire to quest for further information
- to trigger the natural need to make sense of clues given in the source through the construction of stories which flesh out the clues
- to create an appropriate background of concerns and feelings amongst the group.

Stage 3 Possible drama situations and techniques

This stage is mainly concerned with inventing scenarios and forms suggested by, and appropriate to, the starting point and development of the theme.

It involves brainstorming possible scenes and ideas for dramatic exploration. At this stage, the ideas are not developed in any sequence: this stage is about being open to a variety of possibilities generated from the teacher's and students' cultural knowledge of story, TV, film, etc. A 'story' starting point will contain scenes, meetings, encounters which can be used for drama; an image from a story or an illustration or photograph, used as a starting point, may suggest a scene which can be built up through drama. Form is an important consideration. A scene can be worked on in a variety of ways; each way will illuminate the scene from a different perspective. Indeed, the same scene may be profitably reworked in a variety of forms, as mime, as still image, as prepared improvisation, as thoughts of the characters involved etc. (See p. 54 for some useful techniques).

____ Stage 4   Creating an action plan out of ____ the ideas

The ideas for dramatic activity will need ordering so that there is a logic in the sequence that will reflect the objectives identified at Stage 1. Some teachers may decide only on an initial activity and then allow the drama to follow its course. Some may present the ideas to the students and discuss what will be gained from the different approaches. Other teachers may need a 'map' of possible sequences of ideas in order to feel secure.

It's important to sequence the ideas so that there is *progression* in the sense of deeper involvement and deeper exploration rather than a progression based simply on the plot or a linear sequence of events – the students may turn the story in all kinds of directions which will confuse a plot sequence; a sequence based on depth will accommodate shifts in the development of the plot.

The sequencing of ideas needs to take certain basic needs into consideration:

● **Need for the teacher to feel secure that the activity will be controlled and purposeful**
   The suggested ideas will pose different kinds of challenge for a group. The teacher's instincts about the group and what they will be able to manage, understand and feel comfortable with will be an important factor in deciding on a suitable progression. The teacher may want to start with a controlled way of working such as a still image or game before building up to the demands of an improvisation. On the other hand, some groups may benefit from moving directly into a meeting or interview situation in order to engage their interest.

● **Need to establish context**
   The progression of ideas will need to take into account the necessity of fixing context at a number of levels: *physical* – place, time, people, purpose; *aesthetic* – ways of working, techniques and how they work; *emotional* – atmosphere, tensions, feelings; *educational* – what learning is on offer, what questions are being asked through the work. *Clarity over context is necessary for full involvement in the drama.*

- **Need to build belief in the fiction**
  Each student needs to be brought into the fictional world of
  the drama, to believe in its credibility in order to work with it
  as an authentic experience. When the context is remote in
  terms of time, space or culture, work needs to be introduced
  which will help the students to believe in their roles or the
  world of the drama.

- **Need to find/develop the drama of the situation**
  What will make the work dramatically interesting? Is there a
  potential conflict between people, faiths, cultures, priorities,
  class/gender interests? Is there an urgent problem that needs
  solving within constraints of time, money, materials? Does a
  difficult choice have to be made? Choosing ideas which
  highlight the dilemmas posed by these questions will help to
  engage the students' emotions in the work and arouse
  curiosity about what will happen.

- **Need to find fictional tasks/work to resolve the drama**
  As Piaget reminds us, 'Knowledge is derived from action.'
  Drama is speech with action and the ideas should allow the
  students to do more than merely talk about problems and
  choices. The form of drama allows them to resolve situations
  through *action*; having made decisions students are able to
  carry through the required actions and discover their
  consequences. They are also challenged by the actions and
  responses of others. Through this interplay they are able to
  increase their knowledge of human affairs.

- **Need to reflect on the drama as it progresses**
  Learning in drama arises out of the experience together with
  personal and social reflection on the experience – what the
  action means, what it tells us, what we are coming to
  understand about the theme as a result of the drama. Some
  ideas need to be introduced which will lead students into the
  sub-text of the action by helping them to consider the
  psychology of people and situations involved, the personal
  and social drives within the drama, the interests being served
  etc.

The final stage is

Doing it!!